Down Range
To Iraq and Back

Down Range
To Iraq and Back

**Bridget C. Cantrell, Ph.D.
& Chuck Dean**

WordSmith Publishing
Seattle, WA 98168

Down Range: To Iraq and Back
Copyright ©2005 Bridget C. Cantrell, Ph.D./Chuck Dean

All rights reserved

Published by WordSmith Books, LLC, P.O. Box 68065, Seattle WA 98168

Cover art by Norm Bergsma www.incountryart.com
Graphic design by Suzanne Steel, Hot Steel Design, www.hotsteeldesign.com
Information on Sgt. Justin Garvey www.lestheybeforgotten.com
Interior Design by Pine Hill Graphics

ISBN 1-933150-06-8

Library of Congress Cataloging-in-Publication Data
(Provided by Cassidy Cataloguing Services, Inc.)

Cantrell, Bridget C.

 Down range : to Iraq and back / Bridget C. Cantrell & Chuck Dean.
 - 1st ed. -- Seattle, WA : WordSmith Publishing, 2005.

 p. ; cm.
 Includes bibliographical references.
 ISBN: 1-933150-06-8
 ISBN-13: 978-1-933150-06-2

 1. Post-traumatic stress disorder--Prevention. 2. Post-traumatic
stress disorder--Treatment. 3. Combat--Psychological aspects.
4. Stress (Psychology) 5. Psychology, Military. 6. Veterans--Mental
health. I. Dean, Chuck. II. Title.

RC552.P67 C36 2005
616.85/212--dc22   0506

Printed in the United States of America.

~Dedication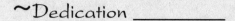

This book is dedicated in honor and memory of Sergeant Justin Wrisley Garvey who performed the ultimate sacrifice in service to his country. Sgt. Garvey was killed in Iraq on July 20, 2003 while serving with HHC-1-187th Infantry, 3rd Brigade (Air Assault).

A fellow soldier who survived the ambush wrote: "He was a man with no enemies...and everything I want to be as a man. Everyone who met Justin was better for it. It was an honor to have served with him up to the end. That night he taught me what a true hero is..."

"Greater love has no one than this,
than to lay down one's life for a friend."
—John 15:13

A Special Message to the Military

As with any book written for a military audience proper honor and respect for your service is of paramount consideration. Since our intention was to keep this work an easy read and to-the-point, we chose to use some general terms in identifying particular units and branches of service. We know the importance of maintaining unit recognition and esprit de corps, and hope you understand that for the sake of content flow and simplicity, we have not delineated between Army, Navy, Air Force, Marine Corps, Coast Guard, National Guard, or Enlisted Reserve. We have attempted to simply use the term "troops" to identify every person for their service and sacrifice. We wanted to take this time to brief you on this in advance just in case we have inadvertently identified you all as only "soldiers". For this we apologize. Thank you for understanding.

** Combat Operational Stress (COS) & Post-Traumatic Stress Disorder (PTSD) **

To date, perhaps more than a million U.S. troops have served in Iraq since the invasion, and tens of thousands have shown some signs of serious stress upon their return. Throughout this book you will not only read about some of these stress reactions, but you will also learn how to deal with and recognize many of the symptoms as they arise. War fighters may or may not return home with what is diagnosed as "post-traumatic stress disorder" (PTSD). Many of the signs of PTSD may be mistaken for what is now termed by military stress teams as Combat Operational Stress (COS). It has been determined that every participant in a war zone will manifest some symptoms of COS (i.e. hyper-alertness, anxiety, frustration, anger, confusion, intolerance of "stupid behavior", sleep disruption, etc.), but this does not indicate that the person has PTSD, however re-adjustment issues are common and to be expected. If they continue to worsen and interfere with the quality of your relationships and with your life in general then take the steps to get support. It is our intent that as you read Down Range: To Iraq and Back you will be able to see that you are not alone and you can use this book as a tool to give you some insight into what is happening as you begin your journey home.

Publisher's Note
This is intended solely for educational and informational purposes and not intended as medical advice. Please consult a medical or mental health professional if you have questions about your health. No patent liability is assumed with respect to the use of the information contained herein. Although, every precaution has been taken in the preparation of this book, the publisher or authors assume no responsibility for errors or omissions. Neither is any liability assumed for damages resulting from the use of the information contained herein.

Note: Many statements, statistics, and testimonials have been extracted and referenced from other books written by Chuck Dean. *"Nam Vet: Making Peace with Your Past"* Multnomah/WordSmith, *"The Book of Soldiers: A Journey from War to Peace"* WordSmith Books.

Contents

Foreword

YOU HOLD IN YOUR HANDS A VITAL TOOL FOR SURVIVAL.
I am on the road almost 300 days a year, training warriors to prepare for combat. I teach the FBI, the DEA, the Texas Rangers and the Army Rangers, LAPD SWAT, the SEALS, and the Special Forces. I have filled up the base theaters at Camp LeJeune, Fort Bragg, Coronado, Camp Pendleton, Fort Campbell, Norfolk, Fort Drum, 29 Palms, and Fort Polk. My books, "On Killing" and "On Combat" are required reading at many military and law enforcement training centers.

This work has proven to be of value to warriors of every stripe—in many types of organizations. With this said, I take what credibility I have and put it all on the line to tell you again—this book, "Down Range: To Iraq and Back" is vital to your survival.

In WWII we lost over 400,000 lives, in both combat and non-combat actions. However, in WWII we lost over 500,000 psychiatric casualties! In World War I, World War II, and Korea, the number of soldiers pulled off the front lines as psychiatric casualties was greater than the number of those who died in combat. Many more had to secretly fight their battles with post-traumatic stress after the war, and most had no idea what they were up against.

Today, we are no different than those warriors of the past. We can, however, be better trained and better equipped to meet the challenges of post-war adjustment. Just as we can be prepared to handle the demands of battle with state-of-the art training and equipment, we can also prepare to survive the aftermath. This is what "Down Range" is about.

As soldiers, we have spent countless years learning to survive the actual battle. Endless days on the firing range; countless hours in battle drills; months in combat learning the "ropes";

physical fitness training every day...all of these were dedicated to ensuring your survival and victory at the moment of truth.   Now, it is time to dedicate some time to surviving when it is over.

PTSD is sometimes called "The gift that keeps on giving." If you die, that is not contagious—but if you live, and come out of the experience with a load of mental baggage, then your loved ones will most likely share in your struggles as well.

Reading this book ahead of time can be a form of inoculation, giving you insight that will help keep your combat reactions in perspective, and help you understand what is happening to your mind and body after wartime experiences. Just as we can equip ourselves to physically survive combat, we can also prepare to mentally survive the aftermath. This book is yet another tool in that equipping process.

Most everyone has heard of PTSD, but not everyone knows about Post-Traumatic Growth. Neitze said, "What does not kill me only makes me stronger."   The Bible says the same thing many times over when talking about how we can grow from our trials and tribulations. As an example, in the Book of Romans, Chapter Five reads: "We glory in tribulations also: knowing that tribulation works patience; and patience, experience; and experience, hope; and hope makes not ashamed."

Some people who never have anything go wrong in their lives can be shallow and fragile individuals. It is often those who have had challenges and trials in their lives who grow the most—they seem to be the strongest in future life challenges.

Seeking help, and recognizing the effects of trauma, is not a sign of weakness. It is a sign of strength, resilience, and wisdom. A sane person would not turn down antibiotics if the doctor prescribed them, and a reasonable warrior would not turn away from psychological help if it is available and needed. As a veteran who has lived and survived in a combat zone, you have had great challenges and tribulations. I hope that through those trials you will have an expectation to be better for your experiences.

Uniquely Qualified Authors

Chuck Dean and Bridget Cantrell, Ph.D. are uniquely qualified to write this book—they have already passed the ultimate test. In

2003, after their visit and work with a unit in Italy that was fresh out of combat, one officer writes: That the instruction and assistance presented by the authors was, "the best program by far".

One brigade chaplain whom they worked with upon returning from combat in Iraq went on to say:

"Chaplain Dean and Dr. Cantrell are two of the most friendly, compassionate, and joyful people I have ever met. Aside from their qualifications in this field, their years of devoted service, and the impact they have had on military veterans, they are a pleasure to work with. They have had a positive impact on those whose lives they have touched."

Chuck's personal experience with PTSD, and Bridget's clinical experience along with her own father's struggle with wartime memories, and their combined years of helping military veterans readjust to civilian life, has earned them the deep respect and gratitude of those who have "been there—done that."

Finally, let me say, if you are a serving warrior or a veteran: Thank you for your service! Or, if you are a loved one of a veteran, or someone who cares, then permit me to say thank you for caring. Study this book well; it is vital to understanding and moving beyond the ravages of war. Above all people, you have earned the right to live a full, rich life.

"He who did well in war, earns the right to begin doing well in peace."

Robert Browning

Hooah!
Dave Grossman
Lt. Col. USA (ret.)
Director, Killology Research Group

Lt. Col. Dave Grossman is an internationally recognized scholar, author, soldier, and speaker. He is one of the world's foremost experts in the field of human aggression and the roots of violence and violent crime. Col. Grossman is a West Point psychology professor, Professor of Military Science, and an Army Ranger who has combined his experiences to become the founder of a new field of scientific endeavor, which he has termed "killology."

Preface

AS A CHILD OF A VETERAN, I SAW FIRST-hand what it is like to grow up in a home with a father who was tormented by traumatic memories. His combat experiences came home with him after World War II and the Korean Conflict, and they became a part of our family for many years. I know what it is like to be a product of an environment where the amplification of emotions run rampant. The intensity of these emotions is more often than not intimidating, unpredictable, and frightening for the loved ones.

Family members living with veterans many times are left feeling helpless and reluctant to communicate. Stress reactions such as these are certainly not conducive to building intimacy and close-knit family units.

Not only do I have a personal experience of growing up with a father who has Post Traumatic Stress Disorder (PTSD), but also a father who was determined to gain insight into his behavior and develop more adaptive ways of dealing with his anger and stress reactions. He has been my role model in confirming that it is never too late to make amends and change the old patterns of one's journey.

Having been fortunate enough to see the world from these eyes, I now devote my work to veterans and their family members. It is immensely rewarding helping them understand the dynamics and effects of trauma reactions. I take great pleasure seeing loved ones working together as a team to overcome the debilitating effects that are sometimes associated with trauma.

It is my hope that this book will offer some fresh new perspectives in developing more effective tools for coping with the aftermath of trauma. Hopefully it will also be a travel-friendly roadmap for your journey back from *down range*.

Bridget C. Cantrell, Ph.D.

Acknowledgments

OLIVER STONE WROTE INTO HIS SCREEN-play of "*Platoon*", "*...those of us who did make it have an obligation to build again, and to teach others what we know, and to try with what's left of our lives to find a goodness and meaning to this life.*" We (Bridget and Chuck) do not take those words lightly, and have dedicated our time, experiences, skills and hearts into making the information in this book available for those who so urgently need it.

Writing it in tandem has been an interesting journey, and it is a product of many life-changing experiences for the both of us. There is no way we can list all the wonderful people who have accompanied us on this writing journey, but there are a handful that need to be acknowledged with much gratitude. They are:

The troops of the 173d Airborne Brigade in Vicenza, Italy who, by their very sacrifice of service, helped open our hearts to the profound needs of those engaged in the current war. Chaplain (LTC) Tom Wheatley, and Chaplain (CPT) Steve Cantrell for their unwavering support and encouragement in our work with the troops. And, Pat, at *Espresso Avellino*, who kept us supplied with hot lattes, and so graciously allowed us the table space for many long hours. Finally, we must acknowledge and give thanks to all the men and women who have returned from Iraq and Afghanistan. Thank you for so openly sharing your triumphs and challenges with us. You have provided much insight that will help stave off many pitfalls for others along the way. Thank you for bearing your souls.

Medic Up!

I THINK MOST LITTLE BOYS DREAM OF one day becoming soldiers. I was no different. As a youngster I played "army" with my friends almost daily, and it became our main after-school pastime. We would run through the neighborhood shooting the bad guys, building forts, digging trenches, and setting up ambushes to defeat the imaginary enemy forces threatening our families and homes.

Having grown up in a military family I was provided with more than a few props with which to play. While living on an Army base in Germany I routinely borrowed my dad's camouflaged helmet, pistol belt, and other odds and ends of combat gear to engage the enemy every day. With everything in place, and a toy M-16 slung over my shoulder, I could step outside and wave at real tanks as they drove by on their way to field exercises. The guys in green always fascinated me, including both my parents when they wore their uniforms. To me they were always real heroes because they served as so many had before them.

A little more than a year after graduating from high school I became restless. I was having a hard time affording college and was getting bored with my life, so I enlisted into the Army. I wanted to join one of the elite branches of the Army and become a paratrooper medic. My interest in medicine and the high adventure of jumping from airplanes was just the ticket—not only did I get a chance to save lives, but I got to wear the same wings on my chest that many heroes in the past have worn.

Two days after graduating from jump school at Fort Benning, Georgia, I went on leave. I was at my mom's house in the Pacific Northwest when she came to my bedroom where I was sleeping. She cried as she told me that we were under attack. I had no idea what she was talking about and rolled over to go back to sleep, but she insisted that I come upstairs and look at the news. A strange excitement shot through me because I suddenly knew that I was going to get to do what every soldier spends his or her entire military career training for—war. The date was September 11, 2001.

I never went to Afghanistan with the first troops to be deployed in the war on terror, but I was sent to the 173d Airborne Brigade in Vicenza, Italy. Day in and day out and practice jump after practice jump, we spent the next two years training. Then one night I found myself on a C-17 transport jet with a parachute on my back and a medic gear bag tied to my waist. We were on our way to Iraq in the opening days of the war.

It was really happening. I was going into combat carrying real bullets this time, and I knew there would be enemy troops on the ground that were going to shoot real bullets at us as well.

We joked most of the flight until they shut down the lights and went to black out. As we started our hard decent to an elevation at which we could jump, so many thoughts raced through my head. I still could not believe it was happening. Half of me was excited to get the chance to be a hero and the other half was absolutely terrified. I kept asking myself, *Can I really do this? Who will get shot first? Will I be able to save them?* I kept running scenario after scenario through my mind making sure I could remember what to do with each injury. Then a strange thought came to me—one that I had never had before. *What happens if they die?* I had no answers.

In the movies the medics patch people up and try to save them. It looks so simple as long as you have the right medical training. What I did not realize watching those movies is that there is a lot of emotion between the two soldiers that is not portrayed in training films. I knew my stuff, but realized that I was with thirty-nine brothers, and did not know if I could keep it together to patch up any of them. I knew I had to—but didn't want to find out if I could.

The first couple of months on the ground were not so bad. However, things gradually got worse. It started with RPG attacks, then rocket attacks and finally I.E.D.s (improvised explosive devises). I.E.D.s are the scariest and nastiest things I have ever seen. They explode out of nowhere and are filled with nails, screws, bolts and whatever else that will tear through body armor and flesh.

I gradually became more and more fearful. Every day was spent wondering if today was going to be *my* day, and if so, would it be painful or would it be quick? When a couple of friends were hit with I.E.D. blasts outside our living quarters, I suddenly realized that I did not want to be in a war any longer. As I looked down at the casualties I was too terrified to move or help, and I stood frozen as I watched people running around screaming, "medic". When I finally went into action I discovered that most of the guys had minor shrapnel wounds. One of them, however, had taken the brunt of the blast and I had to watch him choke to death on his own blood. There was nothing I could do except sit and watch as someone I had trained with for two years slowly die. To add more misery to this, our squad had switched patrols that night with the one who was hit. If we had gone on the normally scheduled patrol I would have been sitting in the same seat, and I would have been the casualty instead of my friend. All I wanted to do was go home. I wanted it all to end, but even now that I am home there still is no end. Not a day goes by that I do not have images of that awful scene.

Not all is bad though. As I recall the images of my friend's death I have also obtained a broader perspective about the fragility of life. I believe it is now my task to find a higher meaning to the experiences I have gone through in my short life. I hope that what I have seen and now know will not have been experienced in vain, and that I will be useful to help others for the rest of my life. I also believe that those of us who survive and live have an obligation to teach others about the goodness and positive meanings to this life. This is the best reason I know why it is so important to support the work of people like Dr. Bridget Cantrell and Vietnam veteran Chuck Dean as they counsel and write materials to help our military make their transition home a safe and sane one. It is my hope that many contemporaries will read and use the information laid out in this book, "Down Range: To Iraq and Back". It is not just a book to read, but a book to use in helping all of us understand what our troops will experience when they come home.

Zech Shone
U.S. Army Medic—173d Airborne Brigade
Iraq - Italy

ONE

Journey from War to Peace

*"Everything looks different in the eyes of someone who
has spent a year in the Middle East…"*
—SPC C. Petry, 173d Abn Bde, 2003

AS BATTLES CEASE, WEAPONS GET STACKED,
and peace treaties are drawn up, it is then that the wounds of the
soul become obvious to each warrior. Just as the captain (Tom
Hanks) in *Saving Private Ryan* so aptly put it in the lull of combat, "every time I kill someone, I feel farther away from home."
People who have not been to war find this statement difficult to
understand.

The young captain-*once a school teacher*-had traveled in his
soul beyond a point that he would never be able to explain to
those who had not experienced combat. His psyche had been
seared beyond a point of no return. The ravages of war had set
him on a lonely journey…one that he would never be able to
share with those for whom he was fighting. His sacrificial duty
had become the vehicle, which carried him to the far side of a
vast social chasm, and the life he once knew would be forever
changed.

Without any doubt one cannot say enough about the deep sacrifices of those who pay the ultimate price by risking their lives in combat. Chancing death or enduring painful wounds by exposing one's body to enemy fire in reality goes far beyond sacrifice. However, as nations engage in armed conflict they ask more from their sons and daughters than just sacrifice. They ask for victory! We arm our warriors with weapons of destruction and urge them to win.

War forces its participants to go beyond the paradigms of ordinary life, pushing them beyond what one would think are humanly possible. When we assertively take the life of another human being we are catapulted far beyond the range of "normal" human behavior. As terrible as killing is, it is still not the worst outcome of war. Cruelty to the souls of the soldiers who fight is war's greatest casualty.

To survive and be victorious on the battlefield, our warriors must aggressively seek out the enemy and kill them. This has far-reaching spiritual and psychological implications. In order to be "successful" the warrior must not miss a beat in pursuing and eliminating adversaries one after another. When they attack the enemy, they are trained to go a step beyond personal moral boundaries and take the life of another human being. This eventually becomes their personal horror of war—this is one primary aspect that damages the soul.

The "killer instinct" that is so energetically thrown around in locker rooms and corporate sales meetings becomes a very real impulse to soldiers in the heat of battle. Without this instinct, the warrior is very lucky—or very dead. Worst of all, he or she may come home feeling defeated because of what seemed like a worthless effort. In any case, the soul takes a full broadside when the mind is triggered and the impulse surfaces to kill another human. It cuts across the grain of everything we have been taught and know about goodness.

At the end of each battle, and when the war is over, the images and sounds of combat are still present in the minds and hearts of those who engaged in it—and these will never go away. Wracking explosions, flowing blood; a burning town; cries for help; and the full impact of what one has done comes flooding back. Now comes the full realization that you willingly participated in something so unnatural to the mind and spirit.

It is at that point, and forever after, that their nation must stand beside those sent to fight in a war. When a nation fails to comfort and accept those who fight for them and engage in the ugly things of war, it leaves those warriors to face their souls alone. This is too much to ask of anyone.

At a time of war we must, as a nation, not allow history to repeat itself. We should never again blame the individual soldiers (like so many did during the Vietnam War) for fighting in a war that was decided upon by government leaders.

Let us be a united country in our efforts to bring peace to the troops and their loved ones when they come home. Likewise, it is not too far-fetched to hope that America will no longer be a nation divided into red and blue States, but one that will be united once again under the banner of the red, *white*, and blue. It is our hope that what we have written here will play at least a small part in this process. Perhaps in these few pages we can bring people together in a concerted effort to help our young women and men make a healthy transition from war to peace. If this happens maybe we can all become the conduit that draws the red and blue together and make a difference for our troops this time around.

TWO

"Mortaritaville"

"Mom, I'll call when the mortars stop."
—Wording on t-shirts at the PX at LSA Anaconda
("Mortaritaville") 90km northwest of Baghdad.

ASK ANY VETERAN HOW LIFE IS AFTER war. Most likely in their own words (and ways) they will tell you how it imprinted lasting marks on their minds and souls. Some may let you know all the different ways their war never ends. Many will not even begin to talk about it because they feel that nobody would ever understand unless they had been there too. For the people back home…they need to understand that it is most difficult to fathom how things have changed for their returning troops. After all, how can anyone see inside of a duffel bag that still goes unpacked? Some troops may never unpack it completely, and we cannot expect them to. The returnees, on the other hand, cannot expect civilians to understand either. Re-adjustment is a two-way street for both civilians and service members alike.

In some ways the war in Iraq is much like the war in Vietnam. One of the primary similarities is that there are no front lines, and you can be attacked at any time— anywhere. "Mortaritaville" is a classic example of that. Let us give you a brief flavor of what it is like:

> The Department of Defense has designated it as Logistical Support Area (LSA) Anaconda, but the troops call it "Mortaritaville". They call it that because it averages more than 50 incoming rocket or mortar attacks monthly, and Americans are routinely wounded or killed by these attacks. Camp Anaconda is near Balad Airbase, which is one of the most secure bases that the U.S. has in Iraq…and it is big. As of May 2004, Anaconda had 17,000 troops and was 12 1/2 miles in circumference. Similar to the large base camps in Vietnam, it is still a war zone—and it is still "down range".
>
> The 4,000 troops in the 3rd Brigade Combat Team, 4th Infantry Division, had nine forward operating bases spread across 1,500 square miles of Iraq north of Baghdad, from Samarra to Taji. The unit was headquartered at Logistics Support Area Anaconda.

(The following is a first-hand account by an individual soldier at LSA Anaconda.)

> "On the night of July 3rd, 2003, American forces were attacked in two separate incidents at Balad Airbase. The well-coordinated ambushes injured 18 American soldiers and left 11 Iraqi fighters dead. The attacks involved typical guerilla weapons such as machine guns and rocket-propelled grenades, as well as a new element - highly accurate mortars that can be fired from as far away as 6.5km. In one attack on a highway near Balad, U.S. soldiers were ambushed three times over a span of eight hours. The guerillas were armed with AK-47 assault rifles, rocket-propelled grenades and heavy machine guns.

Less than two hours before the first ambush, four mortar rounds were fired into the grounds of Camp Anaconda. A total of 16 U.S. soldiers were wounded in that attack. Two of them, members of the 4th Infantry Division, were evacuated from the area and stabilized. The rest were treated on the spot and released. This was the first instance of a mortar attack against U.S. troops since President Bush declared an end to major combat on May 1, 2003."

And the beat goes on.

This may sound like breaking news, but it is more than that; it is a harsh reality lived out by thousands of young Americans serving in the war zone today. "Mortaritaville" is not just a big base; it is a perception. Much like the bunkers, hootches, and muddy monsoon downpours that became perceptions and icons for us in Vietnam, "Mortaritaville" has become a lifelong memory for the troops who serve and survive together.

America's involvement in the Iraqi war is not merely a matter of political rightness or wrongness; it is also a matter of the price we must once again pay in human lives. For the thousands of young people who are fighting, Iraq will live on as vividly tomorrow as it does today. While trying to stay alive at places like "Mortaritaville" troops think and dream of "home" and it becomes a revered memory. Thinking of home, and anticipating a safe place to return to, creates a type of solace that is critical in the mental well-being for those so far away.

Several months into a combat tour, *home* becomes an icon of hope and almost a mythical concept that loses more of its reality the longer one is exposed to the horrors of war. In order to imagine what life will be like when returning one usually resorts to idealizing what awaits them on the home front.

Then the countdown begins. It becomes a process of counting days, hours, minutes, and seconds until one throws down the tools of war and climbs on a "freedom bird" to return home, where it is safe, clean, and comforting. Knowing that the war will end upon returning home…or so we think…gives us peace, however, it doesn't always happen that way.

Those who have been "down range" struggled hard to survive just to come back to the world they knew and loved. We expected to start all over again at square one, but that is no longer an option. The first thing returning warriors must realize is that our reintegration back home will never begin at square one again. Square one no longer exists for those who have gone to war. Home—the place many think is the safe haven to find relief from the stress of war may initially be a letdown. When a loved ones asks, "What was it like?", and you look into eyes that have not seen what yours have, you suddenly realize that home is farther away than you ever imagined.

As a veteran who has seen the hard times, I (Chuck) know I must find a way to make my time in Vietnam count for something more than the heartache it has caused. And I (Dr. Cantrell) as the daughter of a World War II and Korean War veteran, and a thera-pist, who has devoted my career to working with combat trauma survivors, believe that perhaps this is the moment that both of us can offer you a guide and the motivation towards healing.

This book is an attempt to make a caring contribution in sharing our knowledge and experiences in helping those who served at places like "Mortaritaville" come home and find a sense of peace in their minds, bodies, and spirits.

THREE

Driving Fast in the Slow Lane

I went out and bought a fast motorcycle just to feel that high alertness…I need the adrenaline rush because now [at home] nothing really seems as exciting by comparison. There was always a lot of shooting [in Iraq]. When someone's shooting at you it definitely gets your attention and you can never get complacent. I'm home now but I'm still afraid to slack off and relax. The bike helps me burn most of it off, but I don't know what to do with it [adrenaline] when I'm not riding.
—A Soldier home from Iraqi Freedom

"SQUARE ONE" NO LONGER EXISTS.
When you spend hours, days and weeks on vigilant duty trying to stay alive by dodging everything that comes at you, it is impossible to just turn it off when you get to a "rear" area. Coming home is considered to be the ultimate rear area; however, a combat veteran may find life at home to be different than it was before they left. Environmental stressors (sounds, sites, smells, etc.) that were once routine, have now become a combat veteran's nemesis. (Most everyone is familiar with tales of veterans who

dive under tables at restaurants when cars backfire or doors slam suddenly.)

Being startled is only one of many examples of a response to an environmental stressor. The outcome of being on guard or hyper vigilant easily becomes addictive. It is a place where adrenaline pushes the limits and fuels the desire for at-risk behavior. "I don't feel alive unless I do risky things." is a common comment of veterans. One of the veterans I treated was a paratrooper in Vietnam. He referred to himself as a "jumping junkie" because he was addicted to skydiving. His compulsion to find situations, which satisfied his need for that adrenaline rush consumed his time. When he did not have the "rush" he no longer felt alive. Life became comparatively stagnant to what he had experienced in Vietnam.

It is no different for soldiers returning home today than it was some thirty-five years ago. A young soldier I have been treating for his adjustment issues after coming home from Iraq has continuously sought out situations to fulfill his need for the thrill of adrenaline. It is not uncommon for him to find himself in circumstances, which are high anxiety or anger provoking. He has a stress-compelled desire to feel alive in an effort to assure that his adrenaline is activated. It is difficult to pull back on the rush of adrenaline but one must increase their awareness of behaviors. It is imperative to quickly identify whether or not they are putting themselves or someone else at risk by their actions. This will take some "re-training", but it is vital to do this hard work to save a lot of heartache in the long run.

Life at home can be painfully boring. It can seem so slow and seemingly uneventful that we think we have to "cowboy up" to get a rush that perhaps reminds us that we are still alive. Often times this is supplemented with the over use of alcohol and drugs. These two components can lead to disastrous outcomes, which can involve the legal system. This goes far beyond individual risk. In other words, one can easily go to jail now days without much provocation.

This urge for adrenaline may instigate a series of erratic behaviors and activities such as racing cars or fast motorcycles on busy freeways just to blow some of it off. Perhaps even worse, and more dangerous, are the bouts of road rage on these same roads with loaded weapons under the seat. Chasing someone down with flashing headlights and threats of violence because they cut you off can be a one-way ticket to a long prison term. Breaking the law is much easier to do at home than it was in the combat zone. All you have to do is ask the more than 200,000 veterans who found that out much too late, (Brende, J. 1989. & Bureau of Justice Statistics Special Report Veterans in Prison or Jail, January 2000).

I have visited many of America's ex-servicemen who have been incarcerated in state and federal institutions over the years. Most are wonderful people, and it breaks my heart to see these men pay the price for poor judgment. They survived the grueling months of combat only to come home and go straight to jail for the rest of their lives. We are determined to offer tools in this book so this does not happen to your generation.

Driving fast in the slow lane is a metaphor for not being on the same page with everyone else in your environment. There is just something about needing to keep oneself in high gear to find satisfaction and fulfillment in a (boring) civilian world. The only problem is that attitudes, and behaviors, are products of urges, which have no place back home. They simply are not part of *square one,* or even square two, three, or four. When the rest of the world is doing its "thing" by driving in the slow lane, and you are required to drive there also…you cannot run over them just because you are on warp speed with your emotions, and physical needs. It will only get you locked up where you will be restrained and forced to slow down. There are better ways to go about this "coming home" adventure than to end up hurting someone else or being incarcerated.

When I returned from Vietnam in 1966 I had no idea that things would never be the same again. I came home thinking I could resume my life where it left off, and if that did not happen I knew I could always go back to square one and start over. It took me more than twenty years to realize that my quest for square one was futile and that the war had indelibly put its imprint upon my soul. But this book is not about me, or about Vietnam, and then again it is, because this book is about every veteran—and every war; especially you, our young men and women in today's armed forces.

For the boots on the ground, Iraq may as well be Vietnam. The dark psychological fallout from this conflict as recently reported in The New England Journal of Medicine (July 1, 2004) sounds all too familiar to those who remember (and still deal with) the aftermath of Vietnam. When the medical community begins to report "many of our troops are struggling" with deep psychological challenges in Operation Iraqi Freedom (OIF), we can only imagine the magnitude of issues on the horizon. Why do we say this? Because reports such as this from the professional community are for the most part usually artificially low. We also know from experience that it will not only be a problem for individuals and families, but for future generations in America as well. One only needs to glance back and see how the Vietnam War created its long-term complications on an entire society.

Multiple rotations and extended tours have long-term implications for our young service people and their family members. As a society we can ignore the past and be unprepared for our military when they come home. We can choose to disregard and watch thousands of lives be altered in war's wake, or we can be pro-active and take responsibility by arming ourselves with lessons from the past. We currently have the chance to grow up and be the advanced society we claim to be by using compassion and common sense to restore the lives affected by war.

We must attend to those who have been hurt while serving our nation. Their homecoming is a perfect place to start. Coming home from living in a high stress environment is one of the most difficult transitions our military people will ever have to make. It is our task to help shorten that lag time as much as we can. We owe it to them, but the reality is: our job will never end because the process is a journey not a destination. For some it may take a lifetime to make the re-adjustment. We must never give up on our military, we must work and hope for a better tomorrow.

FOUR

Some Wounds Are Not Visible

MANY TROOPS COMING HOME FROM Iraq and Afghanistan suffer from the aftereffects of the experiences of surviving in a combat zone. Vehicular mobilization assignments such as convoys and urban warfare have made this war era unique. Trauma induced by these wartime activities can create vulnerability to stress reactions such as Post-Traumatic Stress Disorder (commonly known as PTSD).

PTSD occurs when a person has experienced, witnessed, or has been confronted with a traumatic event, which involved actual or threatened death or serious physical injury to themselves or others. At which point they responded with intense fear, horror or helplessness. (APA, DSM-IV TR, 2000) The most recent primary diagnostic criteria for PTSD falls into three groups and are summarized as follows:

- Re-experiencing the trauma (nightmares, flashbacks, and intrusive thoughts).
- Numbing and avoidance of reminders of the trauma (avoidance of situations, thoughts and feelings, etc.).
- Persistent increased arousal (sleep difficulties, irritability, anger outbursts, startle response, etc.).

The passage of time alone usually does not heal the psychological wounds of trauma. The natural desire to withdraw from others and not talk about the experiences or difficulties associated with the traumatic event may actually make matters worse for veterans with PTSD. Painful wounds can remain exposed, open, and raw for decades without the proper help that promotes healing. These wounds go on to fester unless they are properly cared for.

Veterans and society can watch physical wounds heal; however the emotional wounds of trauma may go unrecognized if they are never addressed. To continue to say, "What happened in Iraq or Afghanistan happened...end of story," is an attempt to cover up issues and most likely indicates a deep inner-craving (cry) for help.

To recognize that you may be experiencing some re-adjustment challenges is the first step to recovery. Finding useful tools to direct you and your family to constructive ways to re-adjust after war is a top priority.

PTSD Can Happen to Anyone

At one time only troops engaged in heavy direct-fire combat were even treated, observed, or evaluated for psychological problems. But since the Vietnam War, and now the "War on Terror" (where there are no front lines or rear areas), it is clearly evident that PTSD is found both in combat veterans and in many rear-echelon support-type troops. Likewise, it has been diagnosed in sailors who spend their entire tours off the coast on ships. It has surfaced in troops who support the war from static compounds and not necessarily from the front lines, jungles, rice paddies, urban trenches, or Humvees convoying in a hot war zone. Post-Traumatic Stress Disorder can develop in service members who are engaged "down range"...regardless of job or proximity to danger.

To recognize PTSD as a real part of war's aftereffects is vital not only for veterans, but also for the "significant others" at home. Family members, close friends, employers, etc. must obtain as much understanding about PTSD in order to help the veteran thrive in a civil society. In order for healing to begin both the veteran and the people closest to them need to understand and accept that this condition (PTSD) is genuine.

The very first aspect of PTSD that requires understanding is that it is *not* a mental illness. It is a *normal* reaction to the extreme stress encountered during your wartime experiences. It is important to become familiar with the variety of ways it manifests itself after returning home.

Major Symptoms of PTSD

Listed below are some of the most primary PTSD responses veterans exhibit as a result of stress while on hardship tours and/or combat zones. (Tom Williams, Post Traumatic Stress Disorders: A Handbook for Clinicians, 1987, Appendix I)

- Depression
- Cynicism and distrust of government and authority
- Anger
- Alienation
- Isolation
- Sleep disturbances
- Poor concentration
- Tendency to react under stress with survival tactics
- Psychic or emotional numbing
- Negative self-image
- Memory impairment
- Emotional constriction
- Hypersensitivity to justice
- Loss of interest in work and activities
- Problems with intimate relationships
- Survivor guilt
- Difficulty with authority figures
- Hyper-alertness—hyper arousal
- Avoidance of activities that arouse memories of traumas in war zone
- Emotional distance from children, wife, and others
- Self-deceiving and self-punishing patterns of behavior, such as an inability to talk about war experiences, fear of losing others, and a tendency to fits of rage
- Suicidal feelings and thoughts
- Flashbacks to dangers and combat

- Fantasies of retaliation and destruction
- High risk employment/recreation

Some of these post trauma responses may sound or be familiar to you. Healing from PTSD begins with understanding the symptoms. Just by acknowledging these traits can have healing effects for you and your loved ones. The above list may reveal clues that indicate you may be experiencing symptoms of stress. If so, we encourage you to consider addressing these symptoms in a timely manner.

In order to avoid unnecessary surprises it is vital to look at a few specific ways PTSD symptoms might surface in your daily life. Here are some examples:

Intrusive thoughts and flashbacks. Flashbacks are a re-living of the experience as if you are there again by sight, sound, smell, or touch, and intrusive thoughts are involuntary recall of events from your traumatic past that interrupt your normal thought patterns. Daily experiences like the following scenarios can activate flashbacks or intrusive thoughts. Here are some common triggers mentioned by fellow veterans: The sound of sudden explosions, helicopters, or motorized heavy equipment. The smell of human waste and blood, diesel or jet fuel, and dirty canvas are at the top of the list. Driving on dusty sandy roads or along freeway guardrails and overpasses as well as traveling through narrow city streets can set you off.

These examples of actual combat-related cues can be generalized into every day life and living circumstances. These reminders can be as subtle as hearing popcorn popping, cars backfiring, fireworks, people screaming, hot dry days, and even being caught up in large crowds of people. Take a moment and identify what some of your specific triggers may be. Can you put this new awareness into action in order to minimize how you respond to the world around you?

Isolation and avoidance. Withdrawing or isolating from social relationships emotionally or geographically, such as with family and friends can be a major problem. Avoiding activities, places, or people which reactivate traumatic memories is common. If you take on a "leave me alone" attitude it will lead to further distance and heartache. Having the desire to become a hermit by leaving all behind only takes you further away from the objective of re-integration. On the other hand, it is healthy coping to realize that you can only handle a limited amount of social interaction. It may be necessary for you to *regulate* your exposure in order to prevent a negative outcome (i.e. anger outbursts, excessive drinking, etc.). Recall situations in which you felt trapped and needed to leave a social situation. By using good judgment of when to avoid and when to engage may be in your best interest as well as those around you.

Emotional numbing. This is when one distances themselves emotionally from a topic of conversation, a situation, person, or potential trigger which reminds them of a traumatic event. The traits you exhibit may appear to make you seem cold, aloof, uncaring, and detached from those around you. You sometimes find yourself dissociating (checking out) in order to deal with overwhelming feelings and/or painful memories.

The fear of losing control emotionally creates a sense of personal vulnerability. As a defense to this, one closes themselves off in order not to *feel* or respond, and this results in what is known as emotional numbing. You may also have difficulty controlling your reactions, which may result in anger and a desire to solve your problems with aggression. There is a prevailing fear that if one begins to feel too much of anything that they may not be able to control their emotional responsiveness. I have heard many veterans say, "If I start feeling too much, I may never stop crying, and I can't let myself go like that".

We want to encourage you to practice feeling and expressing your emotions appropriately, and when you do, over time your heart (emotions) will "thaw out" and you will learn to feel more comfortable with where you are and what you are doing.

Depression. Is a common PTSD symptom as seen through the act of withdrawing and isolating from others. It can also be a result of situations in your environment that leave you feeling overwhelmed with sadness and the fear that "it" will never get better. You must hold onto the hope that over time it *will* get better. Sometimes it does not get better by itself and remember the "buddy system"...call a friend and have them help. (Hopefully they will be able to connect you with a trusted professional.)

There are certain behaviors associated with depression, and it is good to recognize them. When depressed one can feel helpless, hopeless, insecure, and even unworthy of being loved. Sleeping in excess is also a warning sign of depression. This need to slumber can be seen as a way to avoid emotional pain in hopes that "it" will be gone when you wake up. Sad, but true, avoidance of unresolved issues will never cause them to disappear, and "sleeping it off" is not the answer.

Activities, which used to be fun and interesting no longer provide joy or relief from life's challenges. Your desire to make love can be greatly reduced and intimacy may not be a priority. This in itself can strain even the best of relationships. If your desire for intimacy is diminishing it may be time to get some professional guidance in this area. It can mean the survival of what is truly important to you and your partner.

At this point, you may have realized that you are depressed, and are asking, "now what?" The best place to begin is to seek out and find something to look forward to, no matter how insignificant it may seem. This is called self-care. Some good examples of self-care are: Listening to peaceful music, playing a musical instrument, reading, spending time with an animal friend, involving yourself in a hobby, getting some old fashioned exercise, or finding a trusted friend or family member you enjoy being with. And, as strange as it may seem, just getting yourself up and out of bed, taking a shower and setting yourself on a time schedule will do wonders to get you up and motivated. Begin a new chapter in your life by setting some goals.

Anger. Is a secondary emotion. It reflects a variety of underlying feelings such as betrayal, lack of trust, frustration, sadness, and guilt. Anger is displayed in a variety of ways (S. Akers personal communication, February 03, 2005). Anger can come on without warning, and may leave you and those around you stunned and afraid. The lack of impulse control, such as engaging in "road rage" is a real-time example of how one can get caught up in reacting to what one just experienced in a traumatic event. For example, if you were in a convoy and experienced an ambush or sudden explosion from an I.E.D., then you might find that you use road rage as a form of acting out your aggression. The reason may be, although not justified, is that you have been conditioned in your combat experiences to respond in such ways that you thought helped you survive. However, this is completely unacceptable and dangerous in a civil society. The folks back home may begin to believe that you are "crazy", and you might find yourself making excuses as to why you are *not* crazy. Often these road rage incidences are not even related to the event at hand; it is actually activated by the memory of a trauma you have experienced. Therefore, you revert back to the traumatic event and use the road rage as a means to vent your anger.

Anger can also be expressed non-verbally and be quite intimidating to those who are the targets of your rage. I tell my vets that you have no idea how intimidating you can appear just by your body posture, and your eye contact. To appear frightening and out of control, words need not even be exchanged...therefore you must step outside yourself and look back to see just how threatening your presence and attitude can appear to others.

Domestic violence is abuse. It can manifest in many forms. Whether it be verbal, emotional, physical, or sexual; it is all abuse and not to be tolerated in any way.

Abuse stems from many sources. Low frustration tolerance with a partner or children who have no idea, or reality, as to what you have experienced while you were away, can be a leading cause in domestic violence that can land you in jail. Perhaps you have a mindset that what he or she (partner or children) does is silly and dangerous and not geared for high survival. Likewise, domestic violence is made worse when you add alcohol and drugs to the mix. Using substances to alter your frame of mind only serves to weaken your capability to tolerate the innocent and unaware behavior of someone who has not been in a high risk situation such as combat. Remember, this is another way to end up in jail, or even worse, cause terrible injury to someone you love. If you are prone to outbursts of this nature you must take extra precaution and be committed to changing this dangerous pattern.

Anger is used as a tactic for control and placing "your enemy" into submission, sound familiar? The intensity, the volume of your voice, and the words you use are all forms of communicating your anger. Do so with good judgment.

Anger is a normal emotion, but it must be managed or it may become highly dangerous. However, with the training you have had, and the frequency at which you used anger to propel you into action, you must be aware of the downside of using it inappropriately. Remember, you are no longer in combat and these aggressive methods of expressing anger will only serve to put you at odds with your loved ones and society.

It is also unacceptable to take your anger out on objects or other living things. Breaking things, punching walls, or kicking the dog off the back porch, etc. can only lead to further alienation, shame, and embarrassment. Using aggression in the form of physical and emotional violence can take your life in the direction you do not want to go.

Take a moment to examine the patterns of how your anger is expressed. Is it expressed in the form of remaining calm before the storm? In others words, perhaps your anger percolates just below the surface as a means to mask your rage. Or maybe your anger is explosive and you may even surprise yourself with sudden outbursts.

Expressing anger by creating situations, which are contrasting to your true feelings is called passive/aggressive anger. It is an anger that is hidden away while you smile and say, "no I'm not mad at you". Knowing this, it is up to you to take responsibility to manage your anger. Some suggestions that have worked for other veterans are:

- Physical exercise that is appropriate for your physical limitations
- Reduce caffeine, alcohol and drug use
- Relaxation/study/meditation
- Well-balanced diet and rest

If you cannot do this on your own or with close relatives, it is critical that you get professional help in this area.

Substance and alcohol abuse. Alcohol and drugs are used regularly as a means to "self-medicate" in order to suppress feelings or memories of traumatic experiences. The reason one uses substances may be to numb the pain, forget the memories, relieve the guilt, or to just get away from it all. In reality this is a temporary fix and only serves to make things worse. Your loved ones and friends may think that you rely upon alcohol or drugs too much, and it interferes with your ability to be effective and connect with them. They are right! Your substance or alcohol use only drives you further away from your support unit (family and friends).

If you "use" when you first wake up and if it is the last thing you do before the end of your day, then you should seek help. The next indicator that there is a challenge in this area is when you feel you cannot make it through the day without using. It is important to do regular inventories to see if drugs and alcohol have taken over your life. Reduce your exposure to alcohol and drugs by removing it from your immediate environment. By changing your hangouts, and perhaps even those with whom you associate, may go a long way in helping you get straightened out. Every community provides some sort of recovery program to help those who struggle with inclinations to abuse substances or alcohol. We encourage you to take advantage of the resources that are available to you.

Guilt. You may regularly wonder why you survived when others more worthy died. You may also feel that you do not deserve to be alive, when your buddies were killed or wounded in combat and you were not. This is commonly referred to as "survivor guilt". In other words, you are blaming yourself for the outcome of something that was ultimately out of your control. Some things need to be left in the hands of God.

As a case in point I can share with you my own struggle in this area. In the late '80's I attended the opening ceremony in Sacramento that dedicated the new California Vietnam Veterans

Memorial. As I approached the hundreds of names engraved on this monument I suddenly began to recognize the names of those men that I had trained as a drill sergeant while serving at Ft. Ord, California in the late 60's. I began to recall each face of my trainees, and felt responsible that perhaps they were dead because I had not fulfilled my duty as their trainer to adequately prepare them for survival in combat. I blamed myself and was over-whelmed with guilt and shame. I now realize that after years of harboring these negative and self-destructive emotions I did what I could, and the other variables were beyond my control. I had to release myself from the weight of a burden that I had stuck away in my emotional rucksack for many decades. And now, when I see these brave young soldier's names inscribed on memorials I can proudly say that I had the honor of training some good men in my time.

Suicidal thoughts and feelings. Guilt and suicide go hand in hand. Both can cause us to act out inappropriately. Perhaps you get yourself into hopeless fights or traffic altercations as a means to punish yourself, or provoke (or fantasize) the possibility that others will do you harm (i.e. suicide by police officer, one-car accidents, etc.).

Maybe you sometimes are unable to handle "it" when things are going well, so you attempt to sabotage your success or well-being. This is an intentional setup to fail because you do not feel worthy of success. Relational suicide (intentionally blowing apart relationships with those you love or have committed to) is a very common form of self-destruction with those who have experi-enced war-time trauma. Take an inventory to see if you are insti-gating arguments that are uncalled for, which may give you reason enough to falsely justify walking away from commitments. If you are, then evaluate your priorities and re-visit the value of that relationship, as it was when you first committed. You may be sur-prised to find that you want to preserve what you have at all costs.

If you get to the point were you feel that life is too rough, or that maybe those you love are not able to understand you any longer, and the only way out is by taking your life, then it is time to talk!

(First and foremost, it is imperative that if you feel like harming yourself or are suicidal then get professional help immediately.)

It is very important to discuss the various aspects of suicide. There are a few critical indicators that must be taken seriously. And remember, there is no "*sort of suicidal*"...you either are, or you are not!

Once you take the step to "check out" it is a moment of despair. I have dealt with many veterans who came to that point. They told me that before they pulled the trigger or drove their bike into an oncoming semi, they made a split second decision to live, rather than hurt those they would leave behind. Suicide is the ultimate act of anger.

I have also dealt with the families of those who have actually taken their lives. This is a very painful situation and leaves their loved ones in deep grief. They end up blaming themselves and never seem to get closure for this tragic loss.

If you feel that you have gotten to the "point of no return" and are preparing to take your life by detaching yourself from others, giving away your possessions, thinking there is nothing left to bring meaning into your life, etc. then do not sit on it or carry this burden alone. You must tell someone right away *and* get professional help immediately. Do not leave this serious situation to chance...it is nothing to play around with. Finding someone to share this with can give you a ray of hope in all your pain. It will lighten your burden and open up a new perspective to at least hang in there, knowing and believing that tomorrow is an opportunity to start a new day.

Anxiety and nervousness. An exaggerated startle response is set off by a variety of factors, such as: pop cans opening, fireworks, and other loud noises. Maybe these sounds jettison you into a state of combat readiness. Of course, the use of stimulants and some medications can also create an edge to our nervous system, so it is best to understand how your body responds to a state of anxiety. However, there is a time and place when medication may be necessary to relieve the symptoms of anxiety so you can sleep better and prevent you from getting over-stimulated by your environment.

You can also do behavioral interventions that will aid in lowering your anxiety by doing something as simple as taking slow deep breaths or listening to soft music. In other words, feeding your inner person with soothing elements and becoming more aware of your body takes you out of a state of anxiety. This allows you to anchor yourself and feel more grounded in your surroundings. Finding a safe place in your heart to create a sense of peace will do wonders to quiet the war that still rages within.

Another aspect of hyper arousal (hyper-vigilance) is being uncomfortable when people walk too closely behind you or sit near you in a confined space. After surviving months of guerilla or urban warfare, anxiety and nervousness are normal responses that contribute to generally making you feel suspicious of others. It is normal to feel this way after living beyond the normal range of human activities. It is also not unusual to find it difficult to trust others. I have heard veterans say that they sometimes feel like "crawling out of their skin" when immersed in crowds, public restaurants, or busy shopping malls.

The key to finding good coping for anxiety and nervousness is *planning*. Do what you can not to get caught off guard, or to put yourself into situations that will trigger your hyper-arousal unexpectedly. Develop and practice foresight, just as you would if you were doing reconnaissance of an enemy-held territory. Look ahead, plan, and anticipate what could potentially occur. Ask yourself, *Where will I be? Who I will I see? What will I be doing? How long will I stay? And how will I be able to make the best exit from the situation?* Be careful not to let your anxiety get out of control by blowing a situation out of proportion. Get the facts straight and plan ahead, this will serve to reduce the fear factor which feeds anxiety.

In my practice one WWII veteran shared with me his simple, but creative, method of taking himself out of a situation when he felt anxiety coming on. He mentioned that whenever he was at social gatherings, public places, or even at a person's home he would excuse himself when his anxiety mounted. Even though he did not have a need to use the bathroom, he would find it a solitary and safe place that would allow him to take time out. He could catch his breath and calm himself down before returning to a social setting. This was an excellent means of developing some positive self-care and coping skills. No one ever questions him or his reasons for leaving, nor even has an idea that his anxiety is spiraling out of control. He uses this to effectively manage his anxiety, and it works. Perhaps with a little work and creativity you too will be able to find what works best for you in these types of situations.

Emotional constriction. Is like putting all your emotions into a pressure cooker. Eventually the pressure can no longer be contained within your thoughts. Using the metaphor of "letting off a little steam" clearly takes on a more significant meaning. By letting off a little bit of steam (i.e., physical exercise, hobbies, dancing, traveling, etc.) you are gradually reducing the emotional pressure, therefore making these symptoms much more manageable and tolerable.

Talking about and sharing what is going on with you is an important way to also let off steam…it builds trust and intimacy in a relationship. However, it is easy to just brush it aside, and say, "It don't mean nothin" like the Vietnam veterans did, but in reality they too have developed an understanding that it is important to share their story and to have a witness to their emotional pain.

You will see by opening up a little at a time with a loved one, trusted friend, or a professional that this will ease the weight of carrying "it" all alone. "Humping" by yourself can be a lonely and difficult task, but when you reach out to a "buddy" the process suddenly becomes much more bearable. There is support around you, use it whenever you can to practice telling your story.

There are some things you will probably never share with another living soul. The things you *do* share have now changed you and made you into the man or woman you are today. Allow yourself to think for a moment what it would be like to begin the process of allowing someone "in" to a place you thought would be closed for all time. By denying yourself the opportunity to emote (feel) only sets you farther apart from your community and those who love you.

It is nearly impossible to achieve intimacy with your family, partner, or friends if you continue to hold back emotions because of fear. The fear is often times based on a false assumptions, or beliefs such as: "Once I start crying, I may never stop", "If I open myself up, I will go crazy", or "If my partner really knew what I did, they will reject me and I will no longer be loved". Rather than assuming the worst it is time to take the leap of faith and see how trust does go a long way towards developing a solid relationship. Let some pressure off and begin the process of feeling again; it is vital to survival and re-adjustment into your community.

One of the frustrating moments for veterans is when those who have never been to war ask, "What was it like?" or "Did you kill anybody?" (Yes, this happens more often than not.) As good as your intentions are to share experiences, and for those who ask to hear your story, it may be more difficult to do than you both think. They may not be prepared to hear the stark truth of the horrors and graphic details, so it is best to use caution and temper the words and descriptions you use to convey what you have seen and done. On the other hand, be prepared to deal with the reactions of those who ask these kinds of questions. They may catch you off guard. For example, the soldiers with whom I work have relayed to me many responses from people who have had their questions answered. It can be disheartening when they respond with, "You did that?" or "How could you have done such a thing?" Needless to say, this may be how a person will react to your answers. In doing so, little consideration is given to how their response will affect you. They just do not understand, and this will definitely be a chance for you to practice and exercise a new level of tolerance, and perhaps even forgiveness. They are unaware of your true feelings about your war-time duty and may be shocked to hear what you have to say. Remember, all they see is the person you were before you went to war, and now you are a different person and admitting to involvement in things that shock their senses.

Our topic here has been emotional constriction, and by no means are we advocating that you do *not* want to talk about your experiences. We are only suggesting that you know your audience before opening up. Use discretion and good judgment. We believe that if you do then things will go better for you in the re-integration process.

Overview

Reviewing some of these symptoms so far may have hit you pretty close to home. If what you have read has caused you some discomfort or uneasiness, then it may be wise to put our book down and come back to it when you are ready to continue. This is a common reaction. There is a lot of new information here and we do not want you to become overwhelmed. Remember you are not alone, and your reactions are normal, and we want you to hold onto this, so when times get rough you remember that you are going to make it through this process. It does take time to absorb this and remember it is not about the destination, it is about the process.

Now you are on your way to understanding more about yourself, and realizing that your combat experience has affected you in ways that many will not be able to really comprehend. You have developed some incredible coping skills of survival and self-awareness. Maybe you even look at life as something that is quite amazing, or perhaps you are feeling confused and angry about this whole thing. There can be a myriad of emotions and reactions that can turn on by reviewing this information. We want you to evaluate how you are doing. If you feel you need extra support reach out and find those who can provide more information and a safe place to talk. A good place to begin is the Veterans Administration Medical Centers, and military support organizations such as your base community services. Don't attempt to do this alone; this requires a team effort and support. Just like any military operation…it cannot be done unless you have assistance from the rear.

Warning Signs of PTSD

Stress affects everyone differently. In most cases there are warning signs that indicate a need for active stress management. Check off the signs that relate to you:

- *Persistent fatigue*
- *Inability to concentrate*
- *Flashes of anger—lashing out at friends and family* (or even yourself) *for no apparent reason*
- *Changes in eating and sleeping habits*
- *Increased use of alcohol drugs, tobacco, etc.*
- *Prolonged tension headaches, lower back aches, stomach problems or other physical problems*
- *Prolonged feelings of depression, guilt, anxiety and helplessness*

These are just some of the ways that PTSD may be affecting your life. The emotional and psychological stress of war does not go away simply by leaving it unattended.

The wounds of war do not go away with time, or just by leaving them alone. They need to be addressed, and you cannot do it alone. If you were wounded physically during combat you would allow a medic to attend to the wound. This is no different. Your psychological wounds must be attended to as well. They can be managed with proper help and support.

FIVE

First Aid for PTSD

YOU ARE NO LONGER AN "ARMY OF ONE".
Once you return home it is important to realize how critical it is
not to battle the nightmares, anxious feelings, unexplained anger,
depression, and other PTSD symptoms alone. Many Vietnam veterans came home and tried to "stuff" all their experiences in
hopes their symptoms would just go away. However, most have
found that things only got worse when a solitary journey was
attempted.

So many times in my therapy sessions and encounters with
the returnees from Iraq and Afghanistan I hear them say, "I want
to hear about the Vietnam veterans".

What they are really saying is that they can now identify with
the plight and struggles that have been documented about the
Vietnam veterans. Now that they are faced with the their own
confusions about their war experiences, they can see the value of
knowing more about the re-adjustment issues that came to the
forefront out of the Vietnam era. We feel it is important to review
some of the information brought to public awareness during this
turbulent time in history.

In 1997, I (Dr. Cantrell) conducted a research study of Vietnam
veterans in the state of Washington. I specifically examined how

social connections, length of combat exposure, and homecoming experiences all contributed to the effects and intensity of the veterans' PTSD symptoms. Those who were exposed to combat for longer periods of time, and returned home to negative situations, were less willing to reach out for help. They were more likely to act out their anger, and use avoidance and isolation to cope with their PTSD symptoms. Furthermore, those who did not have supportive people at home, were more negatively affected by their stress. These factors led to a breakdown of the veterans' resiliency to the triggers of PTSD, including criticism for their service. Unfortunately, this did not lend itself to cushion the impact of rejection they experienced from a society who had little understanding for their psychological pain and estrangement. My research study indicates that social support is always a mediating factor in curbing potential difficulties with life performance and coping choices. This is just one more reason why we want to reiterate the important role that family and loved ones play in a healthy re-integration process. (Cantrell, 1999).

Stress affects everyone differently. People find their own ways to cope, but keeping to oneself and trying to handle stress alone is not wise.

Here are some approaches to help you manage negative stress in your life:

Talk it out. First and foremost it is important to find a professional with whom you feel comfortable and has the clinical skills to help. This should be the priority starting point for you to begin your journey out of the dark night of the soul.

If you do not talk about your experiences, and attempt to hold them inside, you may repress bad memories without resolving the issues. This can lead to many undesirable results such as increased anger and frustration.

The fact is that you can only hold these experiences inside for so long before they explode through fits of rage, violence or self-destructive activities and behavior. Like physical wounds that need to be cleansed, psychological and emotional wounds have to be cleaned out before they can also heal.

Next, it is good to realize that you are not alone. There are many other veterans and service people who have experienced similar events in their lives. They are more than likely feeling some of the same anxieties as you. Seek them out and listen to their personal stories. When you are ready, you may also want to share your experiences, and this will help you find a genuine relief from your own stress. There is a certain sense of security that comes from knowing that many service members have probably done similar things during their wartime experiences. This will help you be honest with yourself—perhaps for the first time since the war. Talking it out helps cleanse the wound, and lessens your emotional burden.

Writing it out is another form of talking it out, and can be one of the best ways to sort through, and deal with, many of the issues caused by trauma.

Physical activity. Release the tension of stress by developing a regular routine of exercise. If you have a physical disability, consult a physician to determine what kind of exercise is right for you.

Avoid self-medication. Drugs and alcohol may *seem* to remove stress temporarily. However, in the long run they generally create problems, or behavior, that compounds the stress. Even caffeine and nicotine, agents that artificially create stress-like reactions in your body, can have a negative effect on your ability to control the sources of anxiety in your life.

Learn to relax. Lower your anxiety level and this will work wonders in quieting your body and mind. Learn to think about wholesome and peaceful things and perhaps practice daily relaxation methods. Bookstores, the Internet, community centers on base, and in your neighbor can provide resources for what you may need. Find an activity that allows you to get away (emotionally) from the stress.

Quick Reference

Things to Remember:
- Post Traumatic Stress is a reaction to events that go beyond the range of normal human experiences, and is NOT a mental illness.
- Unattended stress can affect you emotionally, spiritually, and physically. Do not try to deal with it alone.

Things to do:
- Talk it out with a professional.
- Relaxation: Meditation/prayer, art, music, etc.
- Physical exercise.
- Avoid self-medication.
- Join a support group comprised of other soldiers or veterans.

Recovery Process

Some scars are forever, but they fade over time. Emotional scars are no different. There will always be a mark that reminds us of the past experience. One must learn to substitute the emotional impact of that scar with a higher meaning as a result of that experience.

To begin your recovery it is important for you to know where to start. You need to discover how your present reactions and behaviors are connected to the different aspects of your experiences…one at a time. This process may bring up a multitude of uncomfortable emotions and memories.

When you first begin to look at all the symptoms of PTSD you can get overwhelmed and become frustrated. You may say to yourself, I have them all, and then get confused, or lose interest in trying to deal with them because you cannot figure out where to begin. Do not give up.

There are some methods that can help you deal with PTSD on your own. It is important to keep them simple, and remember—it is important to do them one at a time. Step by step. If you find it difficult to use these methods, do not feel defeated. Many people find it much better to connect with a good counselor to help guide them through the issues.

Let me (Chuck) give you an example of a way this has worked for me. It is just a little story about the time I first realized I had become different while I was away serving my country. I was going through the checkout line at a grocery store one day, buying a carton of cigarettes. The line was long, and I was getting edgy with a feeling of being surrounded. When I finally got to the cashier, I wrote out a check and handed it to her. When she asked me for identification I blew up, and spared no words in letting her know what I thought of her for doubting my honesty. Frustrated (and "triggered") I slammed the cigarettes down onto the counter and stormed out. By the time I reached my car I was trembling so much I couldn't drive, so I just sat behind the wheel and clenched my eyes tightly shut. I wanted so much to just make the whole world go away.

A feeling of defeat came over me. I had not felt like this in a long time. Suddenly I remembered a time in Vietnam when a couple of guys got killed on our base camp perimeter.

They had gone down to the dump in a jeep to get some charcoal for a barbeque—and they were ambushed! Here we were in base camp, where nothing ever happens, and the Sarge, along with one of my best buddies got blown away while looking for charcoal so we could have a cookout. I sat on an ammo box and felt so defeated I couldn't even cry. I felt numb. The heat beat down on me like an iron fist. I hurt all over inside and out and all because two dudes got wasted down at the garbage dump—probably by a mama san that we had just given food so she could feed her kids.

Sitting in my car at the grocery store, I realized that I had not trusted anyone since that incident. And here I was resenting a checkout clerk that I thought mistrusted me. *How could it possibly be the clerk's fault? She had a job to do.*

Looking the truth in the eye was tough for me to do, but when I did I saw (and admitted for the first time) that I was not like other people around me. It dawned on me that even simple things that others laughed and joked about I did not find at all humorous. I took life seriously, when I thought others did not. I took things lightly that others held up as sacred. That realization was enough to pull me out of the doldrums and apathetic mindset of a "it don't mean nuthin" attitude that I thought was needed in 'Nam to save what sanity I had left.

The recovery process is just that, a process. It is an evolution of our experiences and reactions. You must make the decision to deal with the issues, and do not do it alone. There are some caring professionals available who have expertise in guiding you on your journey. Talking about the experiences alone is not a substitute for treatment. It is also by your decisions that you stop where you are and try to see things from another person's point of view. It is by your own strength and guts that you step out and become vulnerable enough to even ask for help. When positive strides are made, you are on your way to clearing the minefields on the road to recovery.

Symptoms definitely improve with treatment that may include counseling, medications, and life-skill assistance with relationships, finances, housing and employment.

As we mentioned before, a proven method to help recover from post war trauma is by participating in a support group of peers. This method encourages survivors of similar traumatic events to share their experiences and reactions with each other. In doing so, group members help each other realize that many people would have done the same thing and/or felt the same emotions in similar circumstances. That, in turn, helps the individual realize that he is not uniquely unworthy or guilty—and he or she is not alone. These groups help the survivor develop a new view in relation to the spiritual and physical worlds in which they are a part. This can give an individual the opportunity to re-frame many things and possibly gain a more positive sense about themselves.

Groups, however, are NOT for everyone. Some people do not prefer this method and do best with individual therapy. Groups should not always be considered a cure-all for PTSD.

Treatment May Help You with Your Goals

By receiving treatment for PTSD resulting from military-related trauma, such as combat, sexual assault, and serious accidents, you may be able to accomplish the following goals:

- Identify emotional, social, and physical health problems through professional assessment.
- Reduce the frequency and intensity of painful memories and dreams of traumatic experiences.
- Reduce symptoms of depression and anxiety
- Improve control over anger
- Develop better communication and relations with family members and other people.
- Control of drug and alcohol abuse.
- Obtain restful sleep.
- Increase involvement in purposeful and productive activities.
- Receive medical care for physical problems.
- Resolve financial and housing problems.

SIX

You're Not Alone

Dear Dad,
I've personally blown up five Iraqi tanks in the air sorties I've flown over here. Dad, I know there were people inside those tanks, but I can't afford to think about that right now and still do my job. I know that when I get home I'll have to face who was inside those tanks. I'm not looking forward to that.
　　　　　　　　　　　—A U.S. Pilot, Kuwait liberation 1991

WAR IS SOMETHING SHARED BY MANY, but few understand its aftermath. The reactions to it are common amongst soldiers of every era and nation, and there is a certain degree of peace just knowing that we are not alone. Sharing the experience is the key, and to not do so only makes the problem worse.

Nearly every combat veteran has one thing in common...empathy for one another. The same goes for the families who anxiously wait for them to come home. They understand and identify with each other in a special way. Likewise, most discover a healing relief to know that they are not the only one in the world who thinks and behaves the way they do. When they realize that there are others, even those in wars gone by, who view life in the same way, and then their restoration can begin to take a positive course.

Before we go on with this book we would like to introduce you to some of those warriors from wars and eras in the past. We have collected actual testimonials and placed them here so you can get an idea of how common the thread is amongst those who serve their country in a time of war.

It is our hope and intent that by illustrating these thumbnail commonalities we will encourage you to stay connected and work to manage the emotional (and perhaps moral) issues that your war has produced for you.

Nights with the Demons

Twenty-two years after his last combat experience in World War II, America's best known hero, Audie Murphy, still slept with the lights on and a loaded .45 caliber pistol by his bed. The only problem is, he couldn't bring himself to ask for help concerning his war stress. After all…he had won The Congressional Medal of Honor…

"The World War II generation—we were a tough, uncomplaining people. We were children of the Depression generation who were sent off to war in 1941 to wage a victorious defense of freedom and humanity. We were irrepressible in our pursuit of the American Dream, and entered the combat theaters with a sense of honor and glory that the world had never seen before.

"My unit had its baptism of fire in North Africa. I survived 39 months of sustained combat, and never got hit. Coming home I went back to work at the plant but things weren't right. At night I was having severe "battle dreams," and in the daytime I would go through periods of partial amnesia; I couldn't even remember my own name.

"Since I didn't get wounded I kept my mouth shut about these things, figuring that only the guys who got hit had any problems. Besides, it wasn't too popular to admit that the war had caused any mental problems. I wanted to fit back in and be normal again so I joined a veterans club, not so much for the friendship, but for the opportunity to drink my problems away in the familiar environment of soldiers.

"There was another veteran in our town that couldn't hide his problems, and I tried my best not to end up like him. The last thing I wanted anyone to say is, "He was in the war, that's why he's that way." The people in town turned away and acted as if they never noticed this veteran's odd behavior—after all, he wasn't quite right anymore.

"There were times when I knew that I was out of control, and I would have to take time off work. I was staying up all hours of the night, afraid to go to sleep because of that same dream I kept having. By daybreak, I would be so exhausted that I couldn't even get in my car to drive.

"During these days off I retreated to my own little "foxhole", a small, dimly lit room that was filled with some old relics I brought home from the war. There I would spend time with my demons, and they would torment my mind through the memories of what I had seen and experienced in Africa. Nobody at work ever knew of my problems because I covered it up so well. I never wanted anyone to think I was crazy because of the war. I'm glad to finally be able to talk about it…"

Police Action

"In November we moved within about ten miles of the Yalu River, right at the top of Korea. I was on a forward observers post and saw thousands of Chinese soldiers fill the valley below. As I reported the figures to the command over the field telephone, they refused to believe me.

"Yes," I said, "thousands, sir!"

"Frustrated, I slammed the phone down and watched in horror as the sea of life moved straight for us. The Chinese wanted the Yalu real bad. They pushed us back, slaughtered us, and that bit of war was one of the worst defeats in history. We kept falling back and regrouping, and each time we regrouped, the group was smaller. We had no choice but to fall back because we had no reinforcements or re-supply. It wasn't like when I fought in Vietnam years later; we couldn't call in artillery or air strikes at the drop of a hat.

"We were just out there to face the human wave charges with what guts we had, and the little bit of weaponry that we could pack on our backs. Ultimately, I was alone and became lost from my friends. Armed only with an Ml Garand rifle and a few clips of ammo, I evaded the enemy for three days, trying to get back to our lines. There was only snow, ice, slush, mud, cold and terror, as I made my way carefully past all the North Koreans and Chinese that permeated the frozen hillsides.

"Even though we got a few parades when we arrived back to the States, America wasn't sure if the war was over or not. Things just sort of wound down with nothing to end it except a "cease-fire," and with no side winning. We soldiers knew that we had fought hard, but since there was no victory and just a stalemate, we became a part of America that was put on hold to see "what would happen next" in Korea.

"I was discharged and went silently back to my job. I was as confused as everyone else about this "police action" that we had just fought, and not much was mentioned about it after that.

"At times I would feel some bitterness begin to rise up inside me about the war, and how we soldiers were ignored for our efforts. The best way for me to control any bad feelings and resentments was to work hard in the days and drink a lot at night. My wife and I became regulars at several taverns and dance halls, but my drinking became a threat to our marriage. When I would get drunk I would either become remorseful or belligerent. I would end up crying in my beer, or pick out the biggest drunk in the place and call him outside to fight. I just had too much pent up frustrations that I had to release it somehow."

Comrades of Pain

"When we were in the jungles and mountains the bonds of comradeship were not just in the fighting; it was in the pain that we suffered together.

"When I left my home in Hanoi in 1959 to go south to help "liberate" our brothers, I was gone for fourteen years. In that period I did not go home once to see my wife and family. The time away was very painful, and I cried a lot in loneliness of them. Most every soldier had this same burden. We were alone, away from home; but we were together.

"Many times we were hit with B-52 raids. We hated those planes. They were like death-stars to us. They flew so high and silently that we never knew when we would be struck. Their huge bombs would destroy our protective tunnels, and if we were caught in the open it was devastating.

"Once after one of these surprise air raids our ears and noses were bleeding so badly from the concussion that we were afraid we would bleed to death. After we struggled to find shelter, some of our friends died in our arms.

"Now, after all these years, some of us still get together here in Hanoi and eat, drink and talk about the war. We have a lot of memories, but it makes me think too much about the painful years. I sometimes have bad dreams after our meetings.

"Today I sometimes re-live in my mind those days when we were so hungry that we had to chew on uncooked rice. I also think of when we were so weak from hunger that we could barely run from the helicopter rockets and artillery fire.

"One dream that keeps coming back to me is that I am running in the jungle with my friends. Suddenly, I am alone; my friends have all disappeared. There is the sound of helicopters all around me, and I can hear a foreign language being spoken. Americans noisily break through the bushes coming right at me, and then I am engulfed by blackness."

"Brainoes" Down Under

"The worst thing is that you're still young but can't work; you've got all your marbles up top, but you don't know when you'll have one of these 'brainoes,' so you've got to take life real easy and then you can get by. It's something that's incurable. You can control it, but you can't take tablets and get rid of it like a headache."

"Keith Payne, is the sole surviving Australian Victoria Cross winner from the Vietnam war. Today he finds that it takes the same kind of heroic courage that won him that nation's highest award for bravery to keep his life together. He struggles daily with severe war stress.

"In 1969 Keith served as company commander of a select group of advisors. His unit was primarily South Vietnamese soldiers. In May they came under heavy attack from the North Vietnamese forces, and Keith defiantly held off the enemy, organized his men while risking his life by exposure to enemy fire. Later, under the cover of darkness, he crawled back and dragged several wounded soldiers to safety. Then he led them all through enemy lines to safety.

"The price he has had to pay for his war activities has been dear. Today his nerves remain shaky and he is afflicted with what he calls "brainoes"— irrational and wild temper outbursts. The "illness" started in 1976, years after he returned from the war, and eventually it was so bad that he had to give up his job to live on his disability pay. Today Vietnam is a dark memory for Keith. He doesn't bother with thinking about it, but the emotional scars cannot be so easily forgotten, especially since they can be opened up again with the slightest provocation and irritation." (*New Idea Magazine* 14/3/87.)

South of the Border

"For security reasons I can't say which countries I served in while in Central America. I had planned to make a career of the military until my wounds got me retired.

"For those first few years on active duty I held onto all the beliefs of patriotism and noble ideas that drive most professional soldiers. However, when I started working for Special Operations things began to change.

"In the early 80's myself and another "advisor" had our troops out on a training combat patrol. While we were "practice" patrolling, my point man walked us into an actual ambush. Everything went off at once, and it sounded like the whole world had exploded. My other team member (advisor) was wounded and down. Several others were dead, and the rest of the training platoon had taken off in escape; leaving my wounded team member and me alone. The only thing that I thought of doing was charge the ambush as I was trained, and I guess I went a little crazy. Thirteen guerrillas had ambushed us, and I eliminated all of them within a few minutes. I was wounded and couldn't get a chopper down through the jungle to pull us out, so I carried my wounded buddy 2 kilometers to a pickup point.

"I was very angry that the "indigenous" platoon had run off and left us for dead. I didn't trust anyone the rest of my tour down there, and because of that I still have trouble trusting people to this day.

"In October of 1983, under heavy anti-aircraft and small arms fire, I made the combat parachute assault on the island of Grenada to free the medical students that were trapped there. I was wounded the second day while pulling another troop out under fire. Two days later, after personally killing several Cubans in combat, I was wounded again through the chest and this ended my military career. By this time I was beginning to question quite a few things that the military had me doing. Perhaps the bullets slowed me down long enough to think about it—I don't know.

"I was medically discharged after spending many months in the hospital. However, because so many of my operations south of the border were classified it took me the next 6 years to get my medical records de-classified in order to get the proper care I needed. By this time I knew I had been deceived by the military, and bitterness set in with a vengeance. My physical condition got worse because of it, and my distrust for the government mounted.

"I had been brought up in a church believing that human life was sacred, and now I was faced with the fact that I had done just that—taken another human's life. The thought left me confused. I really didn't know what God thought about me killing people, and I wasn't sure that He would ever forgive me for it. My life has become an array of shattered dreams. If I did all those things for "God, Duty, and Country," then why have I been rejected like this?"

Garden of Tears

"In the fall of 1914 I was part of the Indian 6th Poonah Division that secured the refinery on Abadan Island at the head of the Persian Gulf. Later I was with the units that were ordered by London to strike at the heart of the Ottoman Empire—Baghdad. That decision proved to be tragic for us even though we were victorious in the end.

"A worse place to fight a war could not have been found on the entire earth. We were plagued with every type of disease known to man. The marsh areas of the Tigris and Euphrates rivers were infested with mosquitoes, flies and fleas. All of the soldiers had one problem or another with diseases like malaria, diarrhea, cholera, typhoid and yellow fever. The sun scorched us for ten hours a day, and finally even the fighting had to stop during the summer of 1917 because the temperatures rose to over 160 degrees in the month of July. It was the hottest season in the memory of man, and we were in the middle of it.

"I believe the toughest part for us soldiers to endure was the delirium and mind sickness that many of us came under while in Iraq. Our souls became afflicted because of the dead monotony, and then the repetition of consistently attacking the same ditches over and over, was about all that we could endure.

"It required 350,000 men on duty in Iraq to keep 50,000 combat troops at the front. The Turks always had at least 50,000 fighting against us, but they were a formidable adversary. The Turk soldier's power of endurance, and war skills outweighed ours to the man. They beat us badly in almost every battle, and it was only by strong communication nets, and constant relief forces, that London could provide, that helped us finally defeated them.

"By the time we marched into Baghdad as victors in 1918, we looked more the losers. Starved, ragged, diseased, and sick, we were a dreadful spectacle to see.

"For years after the war I would wake in the night with my body sweating profusely because of the nightmares. I couldn't forget the sight of dying British troops with their mouths gaped open. There was nothing anyone could do to help them—everyone was just doing their best to survive. The "mind sickness" didn't end when the fighting did. It continues long after.

"The irony of it is that the "land of two rivers"— Tigris and Euphrates—is supposedly where God began human life. He planted a beautiful Garden of Eden; it is difficult to believe that that hellhole today was once a paradise."

A Jump into Hell

"In any war there are many important battles…some more so than others. But to the soldier the battles he fights in and lives through are always the most significant.

"The battle to clear An Khe in the central highlands of Vietnam on January 24, 1952 was said to be an historical one—this was my battle of all battles.

"Early on the 24th of January my company, members of the elite French Battalion Parachutists Vietnam, executed a parachute assault landing into the area of Pleiku. From there we immediately made a forced march north to An Khe. There we engaged a reinforced battalion of the 302nd Viet Minh Division.

"I was the officer in charge of 129 parachutists. As we entered the hamlet of An Khe we encountered heavy enemy resistance. Soon after assaulting the enemy positions we realized that we had walked into a major ambush, and the Viet Minh's horseshoe shaped ambush quickly encircled us.

"It was living hell, but there was not time for fear and second thoughts. As a combat leader I immediately assessed our situation and ordered my men to assault the enemy lines to the west. I knew that if we could break through their lines in that direction we would have a good chance of making it to the security of friendly reinforcements at Quang Tri. After much hard fighting we broke through the ambush and made our way to safety in the west. Of the 129 soldiers I started with under my command only 70 made it out alive.

"I went on to retire as a Colonel in the French army, but to this day I can never forget the battle of An Khe. Nor can I forget the faces of the brave men who followed me that day. I'm thankful for the ones who lived, yet sad for the 59 who didn't. Sometimes I wonder if perhaps I'd done something different they may still be alive.

"I wonder…"

After reading accounts from soldiers in different wars as well as from different countries, we can see how it is an experience shared by many. The reactions to war are common amongst the participants, and there is a certain degree of peace each combatant gets by just knowing that he or she is not alone.

The objective of telling you this is to help you come home and get on with your life in a productive way. Sadly, however, many soldiers and veterans believe that by admitting to unwanted feelings or personal problems that they are showing signs of weakness. This is not true, and in fact is just the opposite. The soldier with a problem, but will not admit it, is really only letting the world know that they live in fear—fear that someone may consider them less than who they are. We encourage you to read and use this information in the same spirit in which it was written…to help you live a better life after war.

SEVEN

Down Range Was Different

"The journey home marks the beginning of an internal war for the Marines. 'Give them the space they require to slowly turn the switch. The switch from violence to gentle. The switch from tension to relaxation. The switch from suspicion to trust. The switch from anger to peace. The switch from hate to love'"
— LT. Col. Mark Smith, WISHTV Feb.18, 2005

THE WAR GOES ON.

Many Vietnam veterans have mentioned that they fully expected things to be the same when they got home. However, most have found that the war never ended; it only changed locales. Some have also stated that had they known that the battle for emotional wholeness would continue, they would have been more prepared and capable to deal with life.

Just as veterans from other eras have learned, some of those returning from Iraq and Afghanistan begin battling with the first signs of post-traumatic stress almost immediately upon returning home. However, studies (Army Times 1/7/2005) have shown that the first signs of stress for many begin to appear 3 to 4 months after returning home. This can be attributed to the fact that you are experiencing difficulties re-adjusting to everyday life responsibilities. Your relationships may be crumbling or even failing, and the expectations of those around you are more demanding than you are able to handle. In other words, the difficulties with your re-adjustment can take time to surface, and once realizing that you have changed, and life demands are beckoning you, then the unraveling process can take on a life of its own.

In the spring of 2004, we visited an Army Brigade in Italy. The unit was fresh out of combat in Iraq, and we noted that many of the personnel on post, from top to bottom, had an air of "caution" about them. These men and women had been exposed to sights, sounds, and smells on the battlefield that will stay with them forever. An interesting observation worth noting is that most of them had heard of Post-Traumatic Stress Disorder (PTSD) from parents and grandparents of the Vietnam era. Some had seen first-hand the manifestations and/or problems that it can cause. Others had read and heard about PTSD, and knew what it looked like in real life. Some had even witnessed the effects of trauma first-hand in their own homes growing up. This knowledge alone had caused some tenseness and a concern that they too may have "it". The fact is that many will have stress reactions related to their combat experiences, however, whether or not it develops into PTSD, only time will tell.

Life is different when you are *not* down range, and many of the survival skills you used in the war are not always appropriate in a civilian world. For example, you may feel more secure sleeping with a loaded weapon every night like you did in the combat zone. You may also respond differently now to stressful situations. You may find yourself ducking for cover when you hear loud noises (fireworks, automobile backfires, doors slamming, etc.). You may get nervous or anxious when you hear children playing, crying or screaming, as those sounds may have a negative memory associated with them with the combat zone. You have been trained and have become accustomed to situations that demand immediate action without hesitation or conscious thought. In other words, your response to environmental "triggers" is automatic with little thought to the consequences of your actions.

Home at Last—Finding Middle Ground

Now that you are home many of these particular ways of responding most likely are not conducive to a positive outcome. You are no longer in a situation where it is life or death, black or white, all or none. Choosing to find middle ground in life is never easy; however, it is worth every moment spent on this effort. In order to survive on the home front with your war-time past, this is now your challenge and top priority. It is the foundational structure that transformation and re-integration rests upon. The wise choices you make will assure a better outcome for you and those around you.

Something else to consider is that many changes have taken place at home while you were away. These changes can ignite a new fire and create a different set of stress factors for both you and your loved ones. For example, a person who leaves for nine months and has a 3-month-old child comes back to a toddler who can now walk and talk. You may have missed the first tooth and the first step, and the baby has no idea who you are.

The person you left at home, who once relied upon you, has become quite capable of managing the household by themselves. Many tasks you shared before your deployment, such as decision-making about children, household duties, finances and social activities, have now become the sole responsibilities of the person at home.

Perhaps it will be difficult to relinquish some of these duties. On the other hand, it may be that the person at home wants to "dump" everything back on you (the returning partner). However, you may find that you are not emotionally available to accept these demands. Careful consideration on both sides in reaching a successful balance in redistributing partnership responsibilities is vital in re-establishing a healthy union.

Time can also be a major factor: You may need much of your partner's time that had previously been allocated to others while you were away. Your partner may not be accustom to giving time and attention to you, and may now find that this demand is too much of an additional burden. Likewise, they may begin to resent you because your presence now represents an obstacle in their relationships. Now that you are home you could be considered a barrier that keeps them from spending as much time with their friends (i.e., support groups, etc.) whom they met during your absence. Relationships that were formed while you were away have a high probability of challenging your partnership.

There is hardly anything worse than a failed expectation for both the person arriving home and the person waiting for them to return. You both have your own ideas of what it will be like when you are re-united. Your dreams and hopes have been the fuel that has kept the anticipation of this reunification vibrant and alive. However, this anticipation can have negative effects on you, such as worry, fear, and anxiety. Both of you more than likely have developed different ideas, plans, and projections of what to expect on the homecoming.

These anticipated dreams of what you "expect" of your partner may create areas of contention. Compromise, flexibility and creativity will serve both of you well in finding middle ground in re-establishing your relationship.

A very productive activity is to make a list of the expectations that you have envisioned during your absence. Ask your partner to do the same. After you compile this list go over it and evaluate your realistic needs. Place a check mark indicating those expectations that are unreal and impossible to fulfill with your partner or existing family members. Once you have sorted out the *unrealistic* expectations, or those that seem too demanding, focus your attention on those that *can* be fulfilled. In other words, do what you can do, and avoid chewing off too much as you begin to work through this process.

To summarize, it is important to first and foremost evaluate these expectations in union with your partner. Secondly, it is healthy knowing that you are not alone in dealing with the effects of war, and this can provide a special sense of confidence for you and your loved ones. Understanding and knowledge is always a powerful aspect in the healing process. Lastly, do not let unrealistic expectations "ambush" you in re-establishing harmony with your loved ones.

Yes, your life will be different after war and if you are aware of some of the key changes, your transition will be much smoother. We hope these important aspects help, as you work on your journey home.

EIGHT

Going from One World to the Next

WHEN YOU LEAVE HOME TO SERVE IN the military you are stepping out of one world into another. In most cases you will be thrust into a new environment overnight where adapting and learning to survive with a new set of rules in unfamiliar surroundings is the order of the day. A new soldier (sailor, airmen, or marine) must strive to become a working member of this new life. In the process, one usually develops a new identity within this new "community" setting. You may even acquire a nickname and that is what defines you from that point on.

From day one of basic training, you begin to change, and it is the drill cadre's primary job to facilitate this metamorphosis. Combining this with the tremendous sense of personal danger and stress during wartime duty, it is easy for close family members to see how you have changed. Many of these changes can be alarming for unprepared family members. It is important to know that they probably will not get you back in the same state of mind in which you left. Not to say this is all bad, because you know that many of the changes in you can be attributed to a lot of personal growth.

Back on the Job

Veterans who have experienced war are impacted in ways that make it difficult to adjust and re-integrate back into the work place. These difficulties manifest themselves in various ways. It is common for veterans to feel that they cannot be around people, and many have problems with authority figures. On top of that, they may have a low frustration tolerance and no patience for simple mistakes (stupid decisions and mistakes could have gotten them killed "down range").

Because most jobs require contact with other people, and contain hierarchies of employees, veterans are easily reminded of many negative aspects of military life. Incompetent chains of command are just one pet peeve for most. Too many times inept combat leadership and poor decision-making resulted in life-threatening scenarios and people were needlessly wounded or killed. The veteran may easily bring this deadly reminder into a "normal" work place, and they may find themselves rebuffing directions or "orders" from a superior who has not proven to be a good decision maker.

As you can see, this is not conducive to maintaining job security. A work relationship like this can be detrimental and result in the veteran moving from job to job. Finally, they give up and remain unemployed. It is not uncommon to find veterans who have had dozens of jobs since returning from war. Not being able to achieve this viable level of productivity can affect one's self esteem and intimate relationships.

The inability to maintain relationships on the job has many additional destructive consequences. This can create stress on the family and marriage unit. (Financial security is of paramount importance in sustaining stable relationships. Providing for one's family is a very important aspect of feeling like a worthy and contributing partner.) This stability is often challenged when the veteran cannot maintain employment due to war wounds and/or stress.

Hard to Trust

A veteran once told me that if he did not *distrust* people then he would have to trust them. He went on to say that he just could not trust others because he was not ready to deal with being betrayed again.

Trauma exposure clearly affects one's ability to discern, determine, or perhaps even have the desire to want a "normal" relationship. The relationships, which were formed while serving in the military, were based on the perspective and commitment that one would be *willing to lay down their life for another person.* It is all about trust and camaraderie.

Veterans have shared the deepest of human emotion, terror, vulnerability, hope, love and despair. They learned to bond based on these common emotions, and they formed connections that journey to the very depths of their souls. Consequently, the quality of these associations is unique and has not been able to be replicated in subsequent relationships since leaving the military. This is a major challenge in re-connecting with loved ones.

Inscribed on a "C" ration box by an unknown Marine at Khe Sahn, Vietnam in 1968 were these words. *For those who fight for it, life has a special flavor the protected (will) never know.* In these simple words emerge the very core of connection amongst veterans.

Your partner and family members may sense that you are unable to bond with them at a deep level. There is a time when loved ones feel as if their veteran is putting up a perimeter or a boundary, which does not let them in. Of course, this is may be difficult for you to explain. You may even find yourself saying, "You weren't there, you don't understand".

You must understand the level of frustration family and partners go through by you having an unapproachable attitude. We encourage you to help them understand where you are coming from. We believe that a good place to begin is with agreements and commitments to better communication.

Keep in mind that your commitments require intent, desire, and a mutual vision to commit to another person. Trust is the most important element in this equation. In order to begin your journey in developing trust and commitment, accept and practice the following agreements:

- Agree to avoid (knowingly) hurting one another.
- Agree to acknowledge the validity of the other person's viewpoint.

- Agree to express empathy (understanding what it feels like to be in the other person's shoes).
- Agree not to hide your feelings from one another (be vulnerable with each other).
- Agree not to abandon each other in the face of the worst storms (be steadfast).
- Agree to work out conflicts with each other (finding middle ground on issues).
- Agree to take responsibility for your actions and make an effort to change in order to strengthen the relationship.
- Agree to admit one's faults and wrong doings. Be quick to ask for forgiveness when you fall short of expectations.
- Agree to acknowledge that you are starting from a new point in time—not from where you and your loved one were before they left for their military assignment.

NINE

Home, But Not Really...

> "Happy to be home? On one level, yes, but on another
> it's kind of a letdown. I get so bored most of the time
> that I'm always thinking of something to do that can get
> me up and going. The worst thing is driving. I'm looking
> toward the bridges and the overpasses all the time; look-
> ing at the sides of the roads and the guardrails. Driving
> is different now, and it's really strange to get stuck in
> traffic. No more hitting the gas pedal and jumping over
> curbs, speeding across highway medians or cutting off
> vehicles piled up at an intersection. In Iraq I could do
> whatever I wanted..."
>
> —A Marine home from Iraq

HOMECOMING IS A PROCESS, NOT A
single event. It is one step at a time without expecting it to all go
away. As soon as you set down in the USA it is easy to believe that
your troubles are over, but do not let yourself get discouraged
when life continues to unravel around you. Remember...it is normal to think differently and see life differently after spending a
year in a combat zone.

In making the transition from war to home the very first thing that combatants may notice is that they are on high alert most of the time. Hyper vigilance has become a part of life; it is what keeps one alive in war zones. Jumping at noises, unconsciously reaching for weapons, allowing anger to overpower, etc., can last for weeks, months, or even years after returning home.

You may expect it (stress reactions) to be gone in a month or so, but there are no guarantees that it will just naturally disappear. I (Chuck) expected many thoughts, behaviors, and habits to just go away when I got back from Vietnam, however most did not. Sadly, I suffered along with my loved ones for many long hard years afterwards. I found that these stress reactions do not go away if you merely leave them alone. They hide like snipers in the deep crevasses of our souls, and show up when least expected.

As for the process, we must all remember that our lives are forever changed after war. There is no going back to square one to start over. We need not set an ambush for ourselves by thinking we can go back where we left off. It is important to re-frame our thoughts and notions of what life is like *now*.

It is suggested that families and loved ones learn as much as possible to prepare for the changes in you before your homecoming. We advise that your loved ones consider going through our Phase 1 orientation course ("Hearts on the Homefront"). We have written this course for the purpose of helping them understand and prepare for your return. (See the resources section of this book for more information.)

As a returning combatant you will be different in some common situations. One Army wife said, "Not long after my husband came back from Iraq we took the kids to a circus. He was edgy being around the large crowd and noise. When a cannon was fired as part of the show, he got up and left. He just up and walked out." If the wife did not know the mechanics of his stress, or expect this, she could take it personally. She could become upset to the point of adding more strain on their relationship.

As you can see these types of reactions can be easily misunderstood by those who were "not there". That is a perfect example of why it is important for both parties to be well informed about the various manifestations of stress reactions. For instance, if this wife had known that loud sounds such as a cannon exploding would have a triggered her husband, she could have warned him ahead of time. Or perhaps, they may have even declined to attend such an event. Having this loving and understanding support from people with whom you associate, provides less of a burden for you to pack around.

Boot Straps

People coming out of combat are usually in a hurry to get back home. Often times their first thought is "Let me get back home and get things back to normal. I need to shake this thing off."

I was in mortar barrage a couple of hours before getting on a commercial jet to come home from 'Nam in 1966. Every man in that little compound at the airbase was hit, and seven young men, who had spent a year humping rice paddies, died only hours before leaving for home. I had small shrapnel wounds on my arms, but I wrapped them up and rolled my sleeves down. I did not go to the medic for treatment because I did not want to take the chance of being delayed in getting home. I am not an isolated case either…it was that way with many veterans. We know the same types of situations are happening with our troops coming home from Iraq and Afghanistan today.

Well, "shaking it off" works for awhile, but what you are taking lightly may come back to haunt you in the end. If you begin feeling detached from your feelings and thoughts, this may be a warning sign. You must remember that you are no longer in a military setting. It is time for you to consider reaching out for help.

It took me more than twenty years to admit that Vietnam had affected my life. In that time period I left a trail of broken marriages and families with much discord. This book is written in an effort to help you avoid some of the same pitfalls. I did not want anything to do with the VA for years (thinking that only the guys who were physically wounded deserved treatment). I did not want to be a complainer; nor did I want anyone to know that something was wrong with me. My pride was working against me and I had no idea for many painful years. You do not have to let this be your story. Do not wait to address the issues you brought home.

To hide the effects of the war I drank and used plenty of drugs. I thought that if I acted out while being drunk or stoned people around me would merely think it was the substance I was on, and that my strange behavior had nothing to do with being in a war. I wanted to be a brave, whole person, and not a victim. I was an airborne soldier and knew I could suck it up, but it did not work. Secretly I was always alone…even in the middle of a crowd. I smiled on the outside, but wept on the inside. I used my social "camouflage" well. Fortunately, I did finally find meaning to my experiences. I then sought out professional help through the VA system and it has changed my life for the better.

PTSD is Not Limited to the Past

A large part of coming home is relating to veterans of past eras. Getting to know one another and relating experiences can be tremendously healing. We encourage you to embrace other veterans and find time to associate with them. Therefore, let us not squander all those hard-learned lessons. Veterans should work together now to help shorten the time period for all soldiers like you, by sharing their knowledge and helping you sort out the stressful reactions to the war you were in.

In the past, professionals did not really understand the effects of trauma on combat troops to the extent they do today (T. Schumacher, personal communication, January 25, 2005). Thanks to the Vietnam era veterans who stood up and challenged the institutionalized thinking, we now have a tremendous base of knowledge from which to work.

We know that battle-hardened soldiers are reluctant to talk about their issues. Some of this is because of the risk they take in admitting a problem when it may reflect poorly on their records. If the soldier plans on making a career of the military, this could present a threat of not being advanced in rank. One bastion of confidence that remains in the military is the chaplain corps. Troops generally feel more open to discussing their PTSD issues with a chaplain, not only because of the confidentiality, but because of the non-threatening nature and appearance of spiritual counseling.

The good news, however, is that with the realization that the clinical programs at the VA to address PTSD were designed for veterans primarily of past wars, new programs are now in place for contemporary combatants. (As of November, 2004 more than 8,700, U.S. military personnel serving in Iraq and Afghanistan have been treated for combat-related mental health problems through the Department of Veterans Affairs. These numbers continue to rise.)

U.S. troops returning from Iraq and Afghanistan can get access to vet-to-vet support groups, individual mental-health therapy and treatment (for such problems as nightmares, sleeplessness, depression, anxiety, unexplained anger, and the other stress disorders) through a variety of providers. The VA Medical Center PTSD programs that offer counseling can be found across the country and many territories. For vet-to-vet support Veterans Outreach Centers are located nationally as well. Point Man International is one veteran-for-veteran organization that offers group and individual services as well (800-877-VETS). The Army One Source hotline offers soldiers and their families 24-hour confidential consultation and referral, seven days a week, as well as free, private, in-person counseling sessions in local communities 800-464-8107. (See the resources section at the end of this book.)

New services and programs continue to evolve. For example, in Washington State there has been an effective program in existence since 1984 under the Washington State Department of Veterans Affairs (WDVA). It is so successful that others are being implemented using it as a blueprint by several other States and organizations. For more information contact WDVA at www.dva.wa.gov (PTSD Program information page).

TEN

Asleep at the Wheel

"I could feel the darkness engulf my body, my will, and the very core of my spirit. The unbearable jungle heat wrapped around me and clung like a cellophane bag. I couldn't move; to move meant giving away my position, and "Charlie" was nearby because I could smell the fish on his breath. The dark was black; I couldn't see anything. The sweat pouring from my body was the only thing moving in the whole world.

"What was that? Something close! Breathing! Yes, breathing, and it's on my face. It's time to go for it…it's him or me. Like a striking snake, both my hands shot straight out and clasped the scrawny, pathetic neck in front of me, and I felt a gurgling deep in his throat as I applied pressure. I began to scream, "I'll kill you, I'll kill you!"

"Suddenly, with a jerk, my prey wrenched free and was gone. The light came on, and I awoke to see my terror-stricken wife standing at our bedroom door gasping for air as she rubbed her throat where my hands had been seconds before."

—A night with a Combat Veteran

Nightmares and Sleep Disturbance

Many combat veterans stay awake as long as they possibly can. For them, sleep means another night back in combat. They are preparing for a night of patrols, breaking down doors and searching for weapons. They do this until daybreak; living every hour of darkness on complete alert and in terror of the unknown tactics used by an elusive enemy.

So what do you do? Perhaps you watch late night TV to occupy your attention. You drink jugs of coffee to stay awake and you drink alcohol to try to forget. You smoke to have something to do, and maybe you take pills to shut everything off. It becomes a ritual of "do anything other than fall asleep during the darkness". If you are going to sleep, you make sure the sun is up first. You may even find that after your spouse leaves the house to go to work you can finally relax—and maybe even sleep. With a sigh of relief, you stand down because now *you are off duty*. You see how this works? You were up all night (just like when you were down range) making sure that the "perimeter" was secure, and everyone in the house was safe.

Sleep disturbance is a common dilemma for combat veterans. The nightmares may center on a feeling of helplessness or re-enactments of past threats. Perhaps like running out of ammunition while still heavily engaged with enemy forces, or being a target for a roadside IED.

The seriousness with sleep disturbance is that it brings about a multitude of other PTSD symptoms. Bodies and mental faculties are weakened and exhausted from fear, worry, and anxiety. We lose our built-in ability to rejuvenate through sleep when we are plagued with emotions such as these. With the lack of sleep we become wide-open to fatigue, poor attitudes, rage, intolerance, poor concentration, and depression. We can wear ourselves out. Our bodies will begin to signal us with simple messages through pain, numbness, fatigue, and even crankiness, just to name as few. So take heed and work on restoring the body and mind by addressing these vital issues.

Sometimes medication is the most effective means to get some relief from sleep deprivation…but we are not saying this is the only remedy. There are effective ways for you to be proactive in finding some relief on your own. Stress reducing exercises and activities, and a good diet can go a long way in helping you. Medication is certainly better than living from day to day burdened by lack of sleep, and can be a first line of defense for you. *Do not take up a medicine regimen, however, without first consulting with a medical professional.*

Our last bit of advice may seem simple, but we believe you need to know that it is okay to sleep *whenever* your body and mind tells you. It is perfectly fine to sleep day or night, and wherever you can…be it your bed, favorite chair, in your vehicle, or laying on the beach or front lawn…just do it!

Dread at Night, Fatigue by Day

Going to bed, or getting ready to, can bring about a heavy feeling of dread in you. It is not much different from the feeling just before going out on patrol. The unpleasantness of the filthy environment, coupled with the threat of someone waiting in ambush to kill all comes back frequently in the form of dreams. Once sleep comes, past experiences can be re-lived perhaps by such events as the recent death of a friend, getting separated from buddies while going house-to-house, being hit in a Humvee with an RPG or IED, or seeing bodies being torn apart by shrapnel.

Even though it disturbs your rest, sleep disturbance has its most harmful effects during waking hours. Nightmares, whether or not you have been in combat, can leave lasting impressions throughout the next day. Many people have reported terrible headaches as a result of a dream the night before. The nightmares tend to be inconclusive, and unresolved, and one can sense they are not really "over". So veterans subconsciously work throughout the day to bring these experiences to some kind of resolution and conclusion. As easily imagined, the repercussions of having a terrible dream every time you close your eyes could be overwhelming. It makes both night and day an unreal world of terror, ready to strike at any time.

An impacting side-effect is that spouses of veterans also suffer from their mates' sleep disturbances. Some complain about being frightened as their loved ones shout out commands and cries of terror while asleep. A more serious fear is of actual bodily harm. The partner does not know when the dreaming mate may be "triggered" into a combat mode that might be life threatening. A consequence of your sleep patterns, which may be violent, is that your partner, who has never been to war, may also begin to practice a form of hyper-vigilance. This can be a result of the fear of being harmed by you in the middle of the night.

Simple solutions to this situation is agree to sleep separately for as long as needed, and remove all weapons or threatening implements from your environment.

A Mixed-Up "Time Path"

Tension and anxiety have tendency to sneak up on us when we are feeling vulnerable and can wreak havoc with our lives. Fears, real or imagined, are oftentimes the underpinnings of stress. These fears may be very real, and are associated with mental images on our "time path". Everyone has a mental recording of everything he or she has ever experienced. On this time path we have real fears of near-death/near-pain situations of while we were down range. These situations return to the present in the form of nightmares, intrusive thoughts and behaviors, accompanied with complete scenery and events as we saw or felt them during the incident(s).

On a daily basis we attempt to sort through the items recorded on our mental files just to make sense of our lives. We find that certain high impact events, feelings, and situations stand out and shape our attitudes and senses, and sometimes dictate to us the way we ought to see and react to life. For example, most of us view life differently than we did before we watched the planes crash into the Twin Towers on 9/11. We have mental pictures that will be with us for the rest of our lives.

As time goes by, veterans (those who wear the uniform in their military) may eventually realize that nightmares are related to events from the past. They are based on past experiences and are no longer considered a present-time threat. Our "time path" can get out of order by trauma. The threat of imminent danger for self and others, and the near loss of life and/or limb, can become so great the images reel off as if the events were taking place in the present. When we let our minds go to these traumatic pictures certain responses can overtake us by a myriad of perplexing, and sometimes unwanted, emotional responses.

To Sleep Is to Give Up Control

It is tough to sleep. When we go to sleep, we feel more vulnerable and a loss of control. It may be scary to find that we are no longer in charge of our "area", and sleeping puts us in a place of defenseless against any outside forces, which may appear in the form of these mental images. The feelings and thoughts we associate with these impressions disturb and interrupt our rest.

Many times our mental pictures can be similar or variations of a recurring theme. As with any traumatic experience, these images are lodged in portions of our mind that are not fully available to us on a conscience level. When we sleep, we do not have the defense mechanisms in place to guard against these intrusive thoughts or images. Consequently, very little of the full content in these dream states remains with us, but enough is there so that it has an adverse affect on our lives.

We are "vulnerable" while we sleep. That is why many of us stay awake as long as we possibly can. "Awake" equals control— "Sleep" equals no control. The irony is that by attempting to maintain control of the night (staying awake), we begin to lose control of our waking world. Our bodies were made to recuperate through rest.

Since dreams have a way of discharging mental energy, they become "work" and cause fatigue for many veterans struggling with PTSD. We wake up feeling exhausted instead of rested. It is important that you remain aware of the importance of sleep in your recovery process.

Here are three steps you can take to help with your sleep disturbance and nightmares:

• Do not hesitate to seek professional medical help. Go to a doctor who can evaluate your condition and give you competent, professional suggestions. In some cases, medication may be necessary to help you "cool down" (or rest up) before you try anything else.

- Recognize that your mental and physical time paths do not coincide. One of the best things you can do is to talk about the present with someone else. A sensitive person can help you see and accept that you are probably not in any present danger. Begin to make clear distinctions between past experience and present reality.

ELEVEN

Guilt...
the Self-Imposed Prison

GUILT IS AN ILLUSIVE ELEMENT IN THE lives of humans. It can have negative or positive features that are borne from our life experiences. A positive characteristic of guilt, for an example, is that humans would be void of a sense of remorse if they did not feel bad about causing harm or destruction. We can all be thankful for this type of guilt because it can serve to inhibit a continuum of bad in our world. Feeling bad and taking action to remedy unpleasant consequences is a good thing. Negative guilt, however, can enslave us unnecessarily to many severe PTSD symptoms. The misery of being shackled to memories laced with guilt is a prison that we impose upon ourselves. If these memories are left unaddressed, they will only worsen with time.

"Why did I live when other people died?" "I should have died, and they should have lived." "It should have been me instead."

These are some expressions of survivor guilt. This type of guilt is a way to make sense, or justify why you are the one sitting here reading this book and perhaps your deceased friend is not.

As survivors, we tend to want to trade places with the person who died. Time and time again, we have heard veterans say that the guys who died were the lucky ones, because they do not have to be around to suffer the pain and agony of shame, flashbacks, depression, or nightmares.

You may go through varying mood swings carrying this type of guilt. We can experience a lot of self-doubt, and set out to punish ourselves for surviving when others more "worthy" died during combat.

As survivors, we can go from being quite normal to a low state of depression, then swing into a high state of hyper alertness and anxiety in a matter of minutes; especially if our life situation becomes tumultuous. Tensions in our daily life, such as marital stress, employment difficulties, poor health, and financial worries can trigger these stressors.

The Impulse to Self-Destruct

Many who suffer from survivor guilt lead interesting "flashpan" lives. By this we mean that some veterans may travel a precarious path and even seem to look for the biggest guy in the bar to fight, knowing full well they may lose or go to jail. It is difficult to ascertain exactly how many veterans have taken their own lives in what appeared to be a single-motor vehicle accident. On the other hand, some veterans may feel that they have to "give" all their time and energy away. Others become compulsive blood donors and find considerable relief in giving their blood so others can live.

Guilt is an emotional reaction resulting from an event or behavior that perceives as wrong. Breaking a law or an agreement can send this emotional response into action. Some indicators of guilt are depression, self-punishment, low self-esteem, headaches, chronic fatigue, constant criticism of others, and fear of setting out on new tasks because you think you are incompetent or a failure. Developing relationships can be most challenging, in that you may feel you are not worthy of loving or being loved in the wake of your guilt.

Many have gone to a war zone trained to kill the enemy, but few were mentally prepared for the reality of that action. I do not remember ever being trained to psychologically withstand the shock of taking a life or losing a close friend in war. Sometimes I feel the military expect soldiers to walk through the fire without ever getting burned, but those memories that are forever seared in the mind are impossible to avoid.

Shame

One of the most upsetting events that can take place is for someone to openly and unjustly accuse a veteran of doing something wrong. This has devastating effects on someone who feels they deserve more from a society, or people, they were willing to endure hardships for.

Shame actually triggers veterans into questioning and belittling themselves. It can also produce a great deal of resentment towards the accuser and a self-loathing for the person feeling shameful. The guilt produced by shame and unfounded accusations may lead to frustration and possibly a number of antisocial behaviors and PTSD symptoms.

If shame is left unattended, it festers. The guilt a veteran experiences through shame can cause a feeling of being "used up", and they may become lethargic about life and depressed. It can take a considerable *push* to get them to move freely on their own initiative. Like a heavily laden backpack, shame and guilt can sap one's vitality for life.

Medical Personnel and Guilt

Medical personnel, who get sent into combat to patch up the wounded, and to save lives on the battlefield, often suffer the most painful symptoms of guilt. They were trained for a few months, and sent to a unit to become the "Doc." With a limited amount of medical knowledge, they perform courageously and save many lives. Some of the troops they administer their new skills to, however; do not make it on the battlefield. Many wounded are beyond all medical help, and die much to the dismay of the medic attending them. Consequently, medics and corpsman harbor a great deal of pain and guilt due to a feeling of "incompetence" of not being able to save lives. For these brave men and women, who do their best with what they have, the hurtful memories impact them deeply. Many come home blaming themselves for others' deaths or pain.

Some military medical personnel admit guilt because they develop a dislike for the indigenous people in a war zone where guerilla warfare is being fought. Since it is difficult to identify the enemy, no one, including medical personnel, really knows who is responsible for all the terrible wounds they encounter on a daily basis. When asked to treat wounded Iraqis or Afghanis, many of these medics now live with the guilt of having had less than compassionate feelings for enemy casualties.

For the medical corps working in triage and field hospitals their experiences had its own set of trauma exposure. Many troops, who should have been killed, were evacuated and brought to them for emergency medical attention. They saw soldiers and civilians (who would have easily died in previous wars) live and suffer on their operating tables. Troops with severe amputations, burns, and multiple fragment wounds are living to tell these medics about the horrors of their battles. In past wars, soldiers in these conditions would have been quickly stuffed into body bags and sent home. The medical personnel never would have seen them. In modern war, however, the advancement of medical technology and speed of evacuation methods are keeping more combatants alive than ever before.

As a case in point, I have a friend who served as a nurse at the 93d Field Evacuation Hospital at Long Binh, Vietnam in the late 60's. She was one of the nurses who patched up my unit after it nearly got wiped out on Hill 875 at Dak To. (She was in the Pleiku area at the time.) Our own planes dropped 500-pound bombs on the 173d Airborne (by mistake) while it was engaged in heavy fighting to take the hill, and the casualty numbers were off the chart.

During the course of the action and confusion, she had the ghastly job of tending to the young paratroopers who had survived. They brought the wounded down in helicopters and the dead in dump trucks. My nurse friend tells me there was one thing about the whole episode that sticks in her mind. In her words, "All the bodies were already rotting...the dead and the living."

She is doing better today, but for years she has lived with inexpressible grief, heartache, and guilt. Fortunately, she has found a way and some good friends to help her recover from most of her war-caused problems.

Super Survivors

Many super-active "survivors" use adrenaline for medication. Many take high risks in occupations or recreational sports such as rock climbing, parachuting, or racing cars and motorcycles. Some find exciting relief through torrential sexual encounters with many partners.

As you can easily imagine, living with a combat veteran who suffers from survivor guilt can be a harrowing experience. It is not easy trying to keep up with someone who is running so fast, as to blot out the mental images of past terror, pain, and a feeling of unworthiness. It is a job in itself trying to pin them down long enough to administer help.

Connecting in relationships is particularly difficult with these super survivors. If you believe that you are an "adrenaline junkie", as some 'Nam veterans are referred to, we strongly advise that you consider your position. It is not to your advantage to continuously feed this part of your psychological wounding. For some of you, your obsession for the rush of adrenaline may be a way to feed your ego. It can even give you cause to brag about your high risk behaviors, which can be an excuse for not "feeling" what is authentic or real.

For others, the addiction to adrenaline that served as a necessary survival tool in the combat zone, may now be used as fuel to engage you in workaholic behaviors. Working two or three jobs, long demanding work hours, and filling job requirements that are extreme to the general public, may be a form of denial and a method of distracting you from a painful past. Absorbing yourself in work commitments to the point of forsaking all other responsibilities is not conducive to successful relationships, or a productive re-adjustment. One ER nurse, who had been a nurse in Vietnam and is now working in an emergency room stateside, continues to feed her drive for adrenaline by working many overtime hours each day. She admits, "it is how I know I am still alive, otherwise I would just be numb and not care about life".

Considering all this, and doing all things in moderation, is important to your survival now that you are home. It is our hope that you take time to listen when someone suggests that you are out of control, do not just blow them off. Consider re-evaluating what is truly important for the good of your life and those with whom you associate and love.

Steps to Recovery

Here are three steps you can take that will help you find relief from guilt:

- Your recovery from the guilt caused by surviving when someone else did not, begins when you can separate out the responsibilities in the incident. Proactively direct yourself to think it through. Face your grief squarely, and separate out what is real from your irrational beliefs. You may actually have to list the facts about certain incidents on paper in order to determine what you actually believe about them. This will give a more clear perspective of what really went down. A good idea is to discuss the incident with others who were there with you if at all possible. This too can substantiate the real facts and give you some relief.

  Once you see what is true about each situation, according to the facts, you will begin to discover both positive and negative guilt. If it is negative, it is something that needs to be dealt with. Often you will recognize that the death of someone else had very little to do with whether you lived or died. This task of "sorting out" can bring you to the point of taking responsibility for your past (and present) actions, while at the same time allowing you to freely feel emotions of sadness, anguish, and grief as part of the healing process.

- The second simple release from this form of guilt is to know that it is *okay* to feel sad about the person who died in the incident, and is okay to cry and process through a legitimate time of grieving. It is, however, equally as important to know that dwelling on the incident(s) for excessive periods of time does little to help either. If you find you cannot move forward, it is advisable to schedule an appointment with a professional.

- The third release you can give yourself is to realize that your survival does not make you responsible for their deaths. If you have to blame something for losing your friends, blame the war, not yourself.

Perhaps the most important resource you can use to bind up some of these wounds, and begin to heal them, is to seek out another combat veteran (who is healthy enough to be a safe sounding board) and unload the entire incident. Keep unloading. It is very important to tell the whole story, not just parts of it. Tell as many details as possible. Remembering such things as smells, noises, and perhaps the type of clothing you were wearing. Think back to the other environmental conditions that can guide you into a more precise recollection. Going over your story many times will help you remember more things. As you repeat the re-telling of the experience you will find a growing confidence to open up and tell more.

Recognize that you will probably experience sudden bursts of grief during these story-telling times. It is okay to let it all go. Nobody has ever died from crying. Once you get it out, you will feel much better. When you have detailed your entire story to an understanding "listener," you will find your healing process heading in the right direction.

Dealing with "I wasn't there" (your lottery was not drawn or you served in another theater and not the war zone) guilt is quite similar and straightforward. We have found that much healing occurs when a support vet and a combat vet finally sit down and talk about "their" versions of the war.

TWELVE

Stringing Up the Wire

*"Before I deployed down range I was different about my
wife and kids. Now that I'm back I can only let them get
so close before I have to get away from them. I used to
have fun letting my boys jump and crawl all over me.
We would spend hours playing like that. Now I can only
take a couple of minutes of it before I have to get out. I
usually get in my truck and drive back to the base to be
with my platoon."*

—A paratrooper home from Iraq

Setting up Emotional Perimeters

Many combat veterans must work hard to allow other people
to get close, even their own families. Enduring wartime experiences can cause us to *subconsciously* build a firewall around us.
This self-protective mechanism helps us prevent any more emotional suffering and pain. It is our inner person saying, "I've had
enough!"

We refer to this mechanism as stringing up a "perimeter wire".
It is an invisible barrier of concertina wire used to keep others
away. It maintains a comfortable "distance"…not because you do

not love them, but because you are afraid to bring them into your combat-riddled heart. You fear that if you let them all the way into your heart, and if something happens to them (like what happened to close comrades in war) then the hurt would be too intense to endure, and you may not be able to take it.

The statement, (above) by the paratrooper back from northern Iraq, is a classic example of this perimeter. The young sergeant shared this dilemma with us while we helped the troops in Italy re-integrate after their tour "down range". He came to us seeking answers and wanted to know why he had so little tolerance now for being around his small children. Their high energy had not bothered him before going off to war, but now it was too much for him. He was confused and distraught because he loves his kids and did not understand why he now had this "distance" toward them.

We knew what he was going through. The moment that he told us he *had* to get away, and usually felt best (safe) when he was at the base with his buddies, we saw the reflection of many veterans like him. When we described our understanding of what he was experiencing, and shared something similar examples of what I (Chuck) had gone through after coming home from Vietnam, we could see the relief he needed. I told him about the firewall I had built around myself after I came home.

So how does this "firewall" work? How do we string up this perimeter and put in place such relationship-blocking routines? We do it by subconscious decisions.

We explained to the sergeant that in the heat of battle, or a life-threatening experience, it is common to make vows…and perhaps even bargain a little with God. During times when we witness people (who are close to us) getting hurt or killed, it is easy to decide that it may not be worth the emotional pain to allow people to get close to us ever again.

For many young people, the first time they ever loved anyone beyond their immediate family, was when they became part of a close-knit military unit. They learn to love those with whom they entrust their lives. When these close friends die nearby, the pain is so great that it feels like a piece of them also dies. So to avoid future pain the computation says that it is best not to get close to anyone—and that is the "wire" we string up. It is there to keep us from feeling any more pain as the death and mutilation of war continues around us.

When the war is over our subconscious firewalls are still in place, and we bring it home with us. We still may believe that we cannot allow anyone to cross over the wire to be too close to us. After all, if they get hurt, it may be too much for us to bear, so we make sure that we keep a distant "no-man's land" between us and the rest of the world.

This young sergeant needed to hear this. He truly valued the insight on how this mechanism had affected his life. It began to normalize his experience a bit more. What he needed to hear more than anything else is how *normal* it was for him to react this way. It was a normal response for someone who had experienced what he had over the past several months. Just to know that he was not alone in his feelings, and that others struggle in similar ways, attributed to a very cathartic moment for him.

Some Steps to Recovery

1. Disclose your "wire" to your loved ones. Let them know that it is there, and why it exists. (*It may be appropriate to apologize for making them feel unwanted or pushed away at times in the past.*)

2. Make a conscious effort to allow loved ones to pass over to the other side of your "wire". This will work as long as *you* are in control. It is not advisable to allow anyone else to dictate the pace in this process; you know better than anyone what your tolerance level is to this feeling of vulnerability. Agree with your family that this process requires give and take, and for them not to take it personally if you "kindly" suggest that they back off and allow you to re-set your perimeter. The more mindful efforts you practice, the more successful it will be. Hopefully it will become a healthy exercise for everyone.

THIRTEEN

When a Soldier Goes to War— the Family Goes to War

When a Soldier is Wounded, the Family and Community are also Wounded

Michael Wagner, Ph.D.
Director, Medical Family Assistance Center
Walter Reed Army Medical Center

WAR IS A TERRIBLE THING. WE THINK of war as soldiers facing the enemy in a terrible conflict of hell, bullets, bombs, blood and death. There is another side to war; it is the pain and suffering of the family, extended family, friends, and community that are torn apart from the wounds of their loved one.

This book is written not only for the returning combat veteran—it is written for the families as well. I have passed this book to several family members who have read it and are grateful for the insights it provided them regarding a soldier's time at war. I would like to turn the readers attention to the one's left behind. While, I do not want to lessen the focus from the those who serve in uniform, it is important to understand the role the family plays while their loved one is serving in the military. The families carry the soldier's thoughts, love and hearts when they are at war. They are with them when soldiers are alone through the nights and days of conflict. They are ever vigilant of the fear the soldier has and for their safety. They love them. When a soldier is in danger, the family is in danger. When a soldier gets wounded, they get wounded. *The fibers of their families and their communities are what make a soldier who and what they are.*

Spouses, children, parents and other family members are heroes as well. It is not just the Soldier, Marine, Airman or Sailor that that gives their service to the country, but it is also those that are left behind that spend endless hours, days, weeks, and months fighting the internal battles of separation, worry and longing. The vivid images of war held in the minds and hearts of those left behind generates aches inside with wishes of being able to put themselves in their warriors place to save them from the dangers of war. The focus on the warrior often gets front stage to the point we fail to understand the sacrifice that the family makes when their loved one goes to battle. If you are the one left behind it is all right for you to feel the loss and pain, you have been wounded as well—and, it is okay for you to acknowledge and feel the pain of your wounds. We all feel the sacrifices for liberty and freedom, and as we hear so many times, freedom is not free.

I work at Walter Reed Army Medical Center in Washington, DC where many of the wounded from Iraq and Afghanistan are evacuated to via Landstuhl, Germany. I am the Director of the Army Medical Family Assistance Center. It is our job to assist the families that come to Washington, DC to be with their wounded loved one. We have seen over 5,000 wounded and sick service members returning from Iraq and Afghanistan in the past two years, and over 2,000 families. We assist families in their day-to-day needs while away from their homes across the country.

The US Army Medical Department believes it is important for families to be present in the early stages of recovery. This department has established an operation to enable them to assist in the healing and recovery of their wounded family member. The family's presence is clearly beneficial and contributes significantly to the healing process.

One thing has become perfectly clear to me—*When a warrior goes to war, the family goes to war; when a warrior gets wounded, the family and community gets wounded as well.* I also believe that every man and woman that goes to war gets wounded in one way or another. I believe that the soul gets wounded in every warrior. And, as souls are connected first through family, each wounded soul affects the rest of the system. Just as we as individuals are systems of physical, mental, emotional and spiritual parts that are interconnected; families are systems, communities are systems, countries are systems, the world is a system. When one part of us is out of balance our entire system is affected. For example, when we have a sore throat or broken bone, we do not function as well. So it goes with the family, when a soldier is wounded they are wounded as well!

Recently I was speaking with one mother of a soldier that came home with traumatic brain injury and a lost eye. She told me that their children were affected. She told me that her daughter had been tearing off the eyes of her stuffed animals. When asked why, her daughter said, "That's how people are." Missing an eye had become normal for her because of her father's injury. Children act out and begin to learn new ways of behavior. The little girl that rips out the eyes of her stuffed animals is an illustration of how a soldier's injuries are taken as being "normal", the hidden injuries as well begin to establish new patterns of behavior in the family.

It is because we are interconnected that we are wounded. It is through the love we have for each other that tie us together and we become vulnerable to the wounds of our loved ones. It is in this same love and connectedness that we may find our way to the healing of our selves as well as our soldiers.

And, it is important for soldiers to realize that when they return home it is helpful to understand that their family has been affected. Sometimes, turning outside of yourself and focusing on to the suffering and loss of a loved one can help in your own healing process. Life is different for everyone. It is through our own wounds that we are able to understand, and be sensitive, to the wounds of others. It may be difficult to get past your loss and pain but if you are able to turn your attention to the wounds of others, you may find a special tie that brings you back together.

I participate in weekly meetings at the Mologne House, a hotel on the Walter Reed post. The meetings are for the wives and mothers of the wounded. About twenty women show up each week and talk about the experiences and hardships faced while attending their wounded loved one during the initial stages of their recovery. They talk about the wounds of their Soldier, Marine, Airman and Sailor and they talk about the troubles they have in being reunited and in dealing with the physical, social, emotional and spiritual wounds their whole families have experienced.

Time after time they talked about how things are different. As each speaks I hear the same thing. Each woman is wounded. Each has difficulty in dealing with the situation. Several of them talk about the anger that they saw in their husbands and sons. They are afraid and alone and do not know where to turn. Crying is a very common thing. And, then they talk about the anger they have inside. They have anger at the wounding of their loved one, they are angry at the way these wounds have disrupted their lives, they are angry at how their children and husbands have been affected. Feeling this anger is OK it is real.

One of the mothers of a soldier that lost his leg as a result of an IED (Improvised Explosive Device) blast in Iraq said one day, "I feel guilty and ashamed that I feel the way I do because what my son has gone through is so much more than what I am going through." Other wives and mothers often tell me the same thing. The guilt they feel from feeling wounded is pushed down inside. They believe that they have no right to feel the pain and sorrow they have inside because they think the sacrifice of their husband or son is so much greater than what they are going through.

I don't think this is true. The pain being suffered by the wife, mother or any member of the family is real and valid. Who is to say that one wound is greater than another? You cannot blame anyone, blaming only deepens the wound; it deepens the gap between you and the one you love. You must acknowledge your wounds before they may be healed.

One day after this meeting with the wives, one of the wives came into my office. I had known that she had been having difficulties for some time. Post Traumatic Stress Disorder (PTSD) affected her husband severely; he has severe brain injury as well. She said he has no feelings. She felt the loss of closeness and intimacy they once had. She told me that her husband said that it felt like there was a black hole surrounding his soul. She said that she was afraid. She loved her husband very much but didn't know how she would be able to handle it. I told her that PTSD was not an illness, and that it was a problem of the soul. She immediately acknowledged what I said, "I know." Again, she talked about what her husband told her about having blackness surrounding his soul; she said he felt emptiness inside as she put her hand over her heart.

After talking for a while, she looked at me through tearful eyes and asked, "Is it always going to be like this?" I heard myself say, "Yes." I hated to hear that, and I began to tell her that the wounds will always leave scars, but it will get better.

Months later, I was talking with her and her husband again. She seemed happy. Standing next to her husband, they looked at each other as if they were newlyweds. I asked what was different. She said; "We have been working together with a counselor and they were learning how to face their challenges together." She continued, "This has made us closer than we were before my husband went into the military." They had accepted each other's wounds and they decided to face their healing together. It was a beautiful sight to see the strength in both of them, and the results were even more amazing.

This book, and its course for "Turning Your Heart Toward Home" is one way of working toward reunion. I would suggest that the work be done and involve your family. I also encourage you to read this book together and discuss it as a family unit. In this way you might find the same thing that the couple above experienced through working their recovery together.

I think it is important to be free about acknowledging that family members have been wounded, and encourage your children to understand that they have also been wounded. There is no blame to be made, but rather it is a result of the sacrifice each one of us has chosen.

Briefly, I would like to turn your attention to the sacrifices of the community that we live in. It too pays the price of liberty and freedom. The community can be a very powerful part of healing. The community is wounded when one of its members is missing or disabled. Sending one of our sons or daughters to war takes a toll on the community as it does with the family. If you don't believe this just pick up the newspaper in any town throughout the United States and you can read about the loss and controversy about our men and women sent in harms way.

While the family's involvement is critical in the soldier's healing process, it is essential that the community be also involved. From a purely business perspective we can see the cost on the local community. We loose a productive member of our town or business, and, if we do not attend to the wounds of the returning military it will cost us in lost productivity because of downtime needed to attend to the problem. If the community does not come together with a hand up, the community will pay in the long run in health costs and in dealing with destructive behavior. It is critical that communities come together in the same American spirit of helping our neighbors as in the barn raising efforts of years ago. In the past, when one of our neighbors lost their barn to a fire, the whole community came together to rebuild the burnt barn. Communities must come together to rebuild the lives of those that have served and are serving and for the sacrifices made by them while in the military. As we rebuild each life we rebuild a valuable, contributing member of our community.

Businesses and communities have a responsibility to contribute to the healing of the wounds of the veteran and their family. It is because of the soldier's sacrifice that they have the opportunity to conduct business in a global economy enabled by the liberty and freedom they fought to win. Military members and veterans from this great country have stepped up war after war to defend freedom and liberty for all peoples. Today, each man and woman serving in the military do so because they carry the belief that liberty and freedom are valuable for all people throughout the world.

We are all interconnected and we are all wounded by war. It is through the efforts of each one of us that our families, communities and country are healed.

FOURTEEN

Vet-to-Vet

"Some people say they really, really want to know what's bothering you. So I told them the nightmares, the experiences. And once you divulge, they look at you like you're a rattlesnake, because of what I was capable of."
—A Gulf 1 War Veteran

STUFFING MEMORIES TO HOLD BACK feelings of pain and despair is not a good thing. The "stuffing", however, becomes a full-time job once we come home from war. We can only hold such things inside for a short while before they begin to explode. When they do start to go off it may be when we least expect it, and are not in control of our faculties. The worst part of this is that not being in control is a trigger and a very daunting phenomenon for most combat veterans.

Like physical wounds, psychological and emotional wounds need to be cleansed before they can heal. These kinds of wounds are best purified by systematically *dumping*. Letting it out by confessing the hurt, anger, sorrow, terror, and remorse a bit at a time is the best method, much like a pressure cooker with an outlet valve that regulates your release.

The catch is that veterans do not find many "safe" people to talk to about their experiences, and that is why veterans-for-veterans groups are good. (We must not ignore the fact that there are many non-veteran professionals in the mental health field who are experienced in dealing with veteran issues and war trauma. Their compassion and professionalism definitely make them "safe" communication terminals. I personally have found my group at the VA Medical Center to be very beneficial.)

During the years of work with Point Man International I (Chuck) have also been privileged to see many lives be changed and made stronger through their group meetings. It is encouraging now to see many new outreaches availing themselves to veterans and their families. There are veterans-for-veterans support groups around the country now doing similar work, and we recommend that you look into what they have to offer.

So what are these groups like?

To begin with, the purpose of these groups is to provide a safe environment so you can feel comfortable and accepted in the company of other people with similar military experiences. It is a place where you can freely express yourself and be understood. You may want to talk about the horrible things you witnessed, did, or failed to do while down range. No one will judge you because everyone is there to find healing for themselves amongst peers (no matter what era they may be from). The security of knowing that every person in the group has probably seen and done similar things during the war will help you be honest with yourself and others — maybe for the first time since leaving the war zone. This is a great beginning to cleanse the wounds you may be carrying in your heart.

Jim: A New Guy in the Group

In order to help you picture what to expect at a meeting, let me tell you about Jim, a Vietnam veteran who visited one of these meetings a few years ago. (Some things never change, and the flavor of these meetings will always be the same.)

It was a rainy Monday evening, which is common in Seattle. Our weekly veteran's group had just gotten underway, and the air was a bit electrified by the pounding, monsoon-like downpour that drummed on the small office complex in the northern suburbs. Some of us were remembering the rain in 'Nam.

The outpost leader, Gene, was his usual smiling self. His teeth shone through his Paul Bunyan beard, and he was eager to get the evening started as usual. We had a new guy, Jim with us that night. Jim was nervous and sipped his coffee without saying much to anyone. His eyes flickered from one veteran to the next, searching for a safe reference point. Not knowing what to expect, or what these guys would be like, he had come dressed in a sports coat and tie. Occasionally, he reached up and loosened the tie in an attempt to fit in with the seven casually dressed men around him.

Gene began the meeting by introducing himself, naming his combat unit, when he served, and how his week had gone since we had last met. The introductions proceeded around the table, and there was a good sprinkling of veterans from several different eras that evening. When it came time for Jim to introduce himself, he was a little hesitant. He had served in Vietnam and had never been public about his service.

"When were you in-country, Jim?" Gene asked

"I was in 'Nam from '66 to '67," Jim said.

"What unit were you in?"

"The First Infantry up by the 'Parrot's Beak.'"

Jim paused briefly and then went on, "You know, I don't have a clue why I'm here. I've tried to just forget the war, and I'm sort of thinking that by re-hashing the old memories with you guys may not be so good." He broke off and turned his head to the side and began to sob.

Rich, another veteran, placed his hand on Jim's shoulder. "It's okay, brother, you're among friends. We've been there too, and love ya, man." He reached out and took Jim by the hand and shook it. "Welcome home, Jim".

Jim looked up and gathered himself together a bit, nodding an okay to Rich. "Sorry … sometimes it feels like I got a big pool of something that just boils up inside and then out it comes."

Mel joined the conversation. "Yeah, I know what that's like. I couldn't cry for fifteen years…I didn't even cry when my mom died. Then one time, I went to an air show and an F-4 Phantom buzzed the airfield real low, you know, and I just broke down and cried for about three days. That was right around the time I found these guys, and, well, I know why I broke now, and I've found out that cryin's a pretty good thing. These guys don't mind if I cry in front of them…we all do now from time to time."

"This pool you mentioned, Jim," Gene asked, "what is it exactly? Can you describe it?"

Jim thought for a couple of seconds, and said, "It feels like a slow-motion movie of a bunch of newsreels all jumbled together, and it really makes me sad. But sometimes I get mad too; you know, when I see them in my mind."

"Are there nightmares, too?" Gene asked.

"Yeah."

"What do you normally do to control these 'movies'? Do you have any way to turn them off?"

Jim answered immediately. "Yeah, I drink. Booze numbs me. I've spent many a night sitting in the dark with a bottle of Jack Daniels. It really keeps things from boiling over, and the nightmares don't bother me at all."

"What was it in 'Nam that got you the most?" Rich asked.

"I don't know if I really want to talk about it, okay?"

"That's fine," Gene said, "we can move on. But there's one thing that I've found out in this group, that revealing is healing. Most of us have been down the same trails you have. We've all done some pretty rotten things and had some pretty weird experiences in 'Nam. We just want you to know that it's okay to let it all hang out. When, and if, you are ready we'll be here for ya."

Gene turned to Mel. "How are you doing this week?"

"I'm still sober. It's been six weeks since I went on a binge, but I can't say I haven't been tempted. Whew! It's a hard hill to hump. I do have a little good news to report, though. A couple of weeks ago I had a dream…a nightmare, I guess. I was sitting on a night perimeter in the bush. It was raining, but the air was real misty. You know how it used to get up in the highlands. Suddenly, I could smell the gooks, and I knew if I could smell them, they were real close. Then a trip flare went off, and out of the night, three of them jumped in the hole with me and started dragging me off.

"I woke up panting real hard, and I was drenched with sweat. I got up, and normally I would hit the bottle to numb my brain; I just couldn't go back to sleep for fear that that stupid dream would come back. But I did something else. I picked up the phone and called George there and we talked for awhile. Thanks for being there, George."

Across the table George nodded, but said nothing as Mel went on.

"It was a simple thing to do and just knowing that we have agreed in this group to be on call for each other when things get heavy sure makes life a little easier. After talking to George, I was pretty relaxed and rolled back into bed and fell asleep."

"That's great," Gene said. "Sometimes all it really takes is having the courage to pick up the phone instead of a bottle. That's a pretty brave thing to do, Mel."

Everyone around the table nodded agreement, and Jim seemed to relax a little more because he knew that he was no longer alone.

"I think that's interesting that you had a dream like that, because I frequently have similar ones," Jim admitted. "But I haven't done anything about it except get drunk. I think the toughest thing for me to deal with were the kids over there. What a stupid war!"

There was a long pause. "What about the kids, Jim?" Gene asked.

Jim was silent for a long time. "What a waste," he exclaimed in frustration, and began to cry again.

The group was quiet, but in time Jim began to talk again.

"I was a medic. I was supposed to save lives, and here I was getting off on shooting people." He began to sob again.

"Once in the Iron Triangle I was part of a LRRP team, and we ran into a village that had just been visited by the Viet Cong. The place was still smoking. In the village yard, there was a pile of kids' arms that they had hacked off because a Green Beret medical team had been through and inoculated the kids for cholera a few days before. The damn VC had cut off their arms to teach the village a lesson in not taking anything from the Yankees, including medicine." Jim began to cry again.

"What did you do, Jim?"

He was quiet again, for a long time.

"I went crazy. I lost it! I started shooting every..." He broke again. "I shot a bunch of people..." He slumped forward on the table and let the tears run. A couple of the guys went over and put their hands on his shoulders, sobbing with him.

Gene spoke again. "Jim, you gotta know, brother, that we're in this thing together. There's no way we can pack that kind of stuff around alone. I'm sure glad you are here."

This story illustrates what we mean when we say you need to confess your experiences to get them out. It is not easy. After so many years of keeping the emotional perimeter wire up it is hard to let it down again. But like Jim, and the other combat vets in the meeting that night, you can let it go—if you want to bad enough. It is the healing of our souls by sharing vet-to vet. You will not find a safer place to debrief from your time spent down range.

FIFTEEN

Turning Hearts Toward Home

"My son came home from months of desert fighting, and hasn't unpacked his gear yet. He's still living out of his duffel bag, in the middle of his old bedroom. He doesn't talk as often as he used to, and when he does talk, he's sharp with everyone in a way he never was before. He's different and living with him is more than a challenge."

—A mother of a soldier home from
Operation Iraqi Freedom

THIS MOM WAS NOT PREPARED. SHE BELIEVED that her son would come home and pick up where he left off. Going back to square one, however, is no longer an option. Understanding him and his behavior can become frustrating with no idea how to cope or communicate with him. Left alone, this situation could lead to years of estrangement.

We believe it to be beneficial to spend some time at this point going over some of the dynamics involved in joining the military and then returning home. It may help both the serviceperson and loved ones be aware and appreciate certain changes that need to be recognized and accepted.

From the first day of boot camp, the new recruit begins to change, and it is the drill cadre's primary job to make sure that change happens in order to make a soldier out of a civilian.

Combining life-altering techniques used in boot camp, with the tremendous personal danger and stress of wartime duty, it is easy to see the change in a person who has served in the Armed Forces. This can be alarming for unprepared family members. By accepting the reality that they will not get their loved one back exactly in the same state of mind in which they left. The sooner they have this realization, the smoother the process moves in a therapeutic direction.

Those called to fight in a war are forever changed by what they see, what they do, and what they did *not* do. In many ways, those who come home will never be the same again. When one enters the world of trauma, profound changes sometimes take place. It is important not only for the veteran, but for their loved ones as well, to discover what those changes are.

Many veterans' partners and family members feel that something has captured their loved one's soul. He or she does not seem "present" enough in thought and spirit to devote themselves to the close relationship they once had. The one who went off to war is often distracted and caught up in vivid memories of their wartime experiences. Until they can sort through and gain some tools to deal with their issues, they may spend much of their time thinking about the past, rather than loving the ones who need them the most.

Where did my loved one go, and how do I get them back? is the question that families need to get answered. In our workbook course "Turning Your Heart Toward Home" we have designed some special exercises to assist both families and veterans alike. They are put together to help everyone understand and develop skillful tools to rebuild the relationships that have waned in the wake of war.

Preparing to Reunite with Your Loved Ones

Clearly, trauma has a profound effect on the re-entry process, and re-acquainting with those we love. It alters our ability to clearly see what is in front of us. It also prevents us from objectively evaluating the reality of life's situations. In other words, one's image, or belief about oneself, or others and their world, has been transformed by a sudden unexpected traumatic event. When this happens the very foundation from which to understand one's world and meaning, has been forever changed by one moment in time.

There is hardly anything worse than a failed expectation. The person waiting at home, *and* the person waiting to come home, have their own ideas as to what it will be like when they are reunited. Their dreams and hopes have been the fuel that has kept the anticipation of their reunification vibrant and alive. However, this anticipation most likely will have negative effects such as worry, fear, and anxiety. Life has changed for both the person at home and for the one returning. Both parties may have developed different habits and patterns while being separated.

Here are some examples of these changes:

Time can be a major factor: The returning service person may demand much of their stay-at-home partner's time. The stay-at-home partner may begin to resent not being able to spend as much time with the newfound friends they made during their partner's absence. They may even begin to miss the support network they were a part of while their loved one was away. Relationships that have been formed in the absence of their partner (while they were serving abroad) could seriously challenge their foundation for marriage.

The person at home more than likely has developed an independent view of life. Many tasks that were shared before the deployment, such as decision-making about children, household duties, finances and social activities have now become the sole responsibilities of the stay-at-home person.

Perhaps it will be difficult to relinquish some of these duties. On the other hand, it may be that the person at home wants to "dump" everything back on the returning partner. However, the returnee may not be emotionally available to accept these demands.

At this point, you may be asking yourself, *Is the war experience going to block or hinder our intimate activities?* To answer, it is best to understand some mechanics regarding this aspect of relationships after war.

It is not unusual for people to have a startle response when caught by surprise. People who have had military training or been in a military conflict may be quite vulnerable to sudden and unexpected turmoil or noise. A startle response is an involuntary reaction to a stimulus, which causes a person to retreat or attack without conscious thought. It has been shown throughout the centuries that war veterans have reacted with startle responses under stress even in civilian environments, and this leads to fear and rejection. It has even caused many relationships to end. For example, a veteran may be startled in his sleep and inadvertently attack their partner lying beside them.

If this is a possibility in your relationship, here are some important safety precautions that will help you cope:

- Ensure that any weapons are secured in areas other than where the veteran lives and sleeps.
- Choose and agree on separate sleeping quarters (private bedrooms) if sleeping in close proximity becomes problematic.
- Do not argue or engage in upsetting dialogue before bedtime. ("Don't let the sun go down on your anger..."). Do what you possibly can to resolve, or put at bay, any disagreement or heated discussions before retiring.

It is sometimes difficult for a person to make the transition from war to peace. Intimacy is the essence of peace with another person, and therefore finds itself on the far end of the spectrum from a war zone.

An important question most likely will be, "Will our sexual relationship be different?" This may be a difficult area to address, but understanding the needs of each partner is important to a successful outcome.

The reunion rarely goes as expected, and the events you have been waiting for may not turn out as anticipated. Many times, we are so caught up in the moment, and wanting "it" to be perfect, that we try to encapsulate all our dreams into a short period of time. When this does not materialize as we have planned the impossibility becomes apparent and we realize that we have set ourselves up for a jolting disappointment.

Flexibility and creativity in the reunification are pivotal in restoring the level of intimacy that you both desire.

Here are some steps to help you create a smoother landing for achieving normalcy in your relationship:

- Lower activity level—Do not make plans to accomplish all your dreams in the first few days of the loved one's return— Unplug the phone and focus on each other.
- Create the flavor of a get-away vacation—Keep it simple and easy-going.
- If you have children—Arrange for relatives or friends to keep them for a few days.
- Capitalize on your loved one's favorites—Food, music, activities, entertainment, etc.
- Sexual connection—Pace yourself. Find pleasure in rediscovering one another's personal desires.

Being deprived of intimacy for long months may present a variety of emotions. Uncertainty of their partner's commitment and a sense of longing and anticipation are among the many apprehensions and hesitations that couples face upon reunification. These dreams and desires of the comfort and glow of intimacy can easily be shattered because of what each person has experienced during their separation.

According to Matsakis (1992) it has been established that the single most important predictor of who develops long-term PTSD, or other traumatic reactions, is the one with the inability to derive comfort from another human being. Also in agreement with this perspective is van der Kolk (1988b) who refers to primary traits that can reduce the negative effects of trauma: these are the presence of a support system and a strong belief system that is positive and allows you to trust, set boundaries, and be intimate. Re-integrating with loved ones is a vital step in coming home.

Finding Middle Ground— Resolving Conflicts

One aspect lacking in military training is providing skills for individuals to negotiate conflicts with the enemy. (This is usually left up to the politicians). In the absence of this vital social skill, military personnel often view their partners or loved ones as the "enemy" when encountering simple conflicts at home. It is typical for veterans to either fight or flee in the face of adversity. They have been conditioned by their training to have this strong impulse to survive.

It is vital to understand how conflicts are resolved in a positive, nurturing way. The following steps will help make this possible.

Steps to Resolving Conflicts:

1. First, identify and define the conflict. Who are the participants?
2. Now, create a list consisting of 5 or 6 possible outcomes that you would like to see transpire.
3. Compare your lists and determine which solutions would lead you to middle ground. Which one would ultimately take you to the desired and mutually agreed upon resolution?
4. Taking responsibility for your actions and acknowledging your mistakes is an important step leading to forgiveness and complete reconciliation. This requires an act of laying down our arms, which is not always easy for military personnel to do. They were taught to never surrender to the enemy. The first step in overcoming this is to understand they are no longer at war. Take responsibility to understand where you are. Now that you are home with your love, remember that you are no longer in the combat zone. It is okay to give in so you can mold the relationship you desire.
5. Describe in writing what your part is in taking responsibility for a better relationship. Now put it into action.

6. Pre-arrange with your partner to further your dialogue. Choose an uninterrupted block of time in a mutually safe and quiet location. Discover any transgressions or offenses that may exist in your relationship. Look for behaviors and expressions of emotions that have may have caused problems in your connection. Admit your shortcomings. Apologize and ask for forgiveness.

Self-Care for Leaders

With Tools to Help the Troops

IT IS COMMON FOR WARTIME MILITARY officers to shoulder responsibilities for situations that go beyond their control to manage. When military leaders face the reality that they may not be able to prevent suffering, pain and/or death amongst the ranks they command, emotional stress can result. Unwarranted guilt or shame for the inability to avert that pain and grief can make leaders feel as though they failed the troops who put their confidence in their leadership skills.

There is an old saying, "we can't let 'em see us sweat", and stressed military officers can assume this posture while maintaining a sense of imperviousness around the troops. When they do, their own psychological difficulties heighten and the stress can manifest through many symptoms.

Typically, the first thing a leader may do is shut down and attempt to stuff the experiences, hoping the feelings will just go away and they can get on with their jobs. However, by trying to sweep it away stress reactions only get worse. The question remains, "who" does the person-on-top-of-the-totem-pole confide in when it begins to interfere with their normal daily life?

This is where peer-interaction and debriefing becomes vital. Talking to one another, plus being honest with thoughts and feelings, is a good first step. Secondly, working with a "safe" person, and then learning how to reciprocate by being a listening ear for a peer.

Normalization

It is important to fully understand that there are many circumstances in which we have little control, and these circumstances arise frequently while engaged in a war zone. This is why it is imperative to understand what "normal responses" to uncontrollable or abnormal circumstances may be; these responses provide us with defenses against acute and debilitating reactions when direct control is not possible. In war, it is difficult (nearly impossible) to control pain, fear, grief, death, and the myriad of other human reactions in the experience. Leaders should fully understand that it is normal not to be able to control these things—and to have these feelings. What is happening is not out of the ordinary for returnees from a war zone.

Resolving post-combat trauma is similar to the loss of a loved one. It involves moving in stages through a grief process and can look similar to Kubler Ross's theory on Death and Dying: (1) The impact phase encompasses the initial shock of the incident—numbness, or denial and anger at oneself, and/or at the overall conflict, may ensue; (2) a bargaining process in which basic values are sorted out and self-doubt emerges; (3) heightened anxiety, coupled with a need to isolate, or may be a time that one is compelled to engage in high risk behaviors which potentially could be life threatening; (4) feeling blue and depressed (hopeless/helpless) can set in, and eventually (5) it is to be hoped, that acceptance of your experience and the confidence to regulate your reactions and emotions may result.

Understanding the above points by military leaders is the first step in taking care of themselves.

The following is a self-care checklist to assist military leaders in taking positive steps to a healthy re-entry from a combat zone.

Self-Care Checklist:

- Limit exposure to traumatic information (which includes watching the news, reading the paper, etc.)
- Debrief with peer or professional
- Plenty of sleep and rest
- Diet (3 meals a day—especially breakfast—Reduce sugar, processed white flour and animal fats)
- PT (Physical exercise is crucial in reducing the effects of stress)
- Decrease other unhealthy behaviors
- Limit alcohol, caffeine, nicotine, and illegal substances
- Get addictions under control
- Engage in healthy, pleasurable activities
- Write about the feelings and reactions to your experiences
- Read
- Play/listen to music
- Family activities
- Engage in hobbies
- Focus outside one's self and give back to the community (Volunteer work, etc.)
- Spiritual fulfillment through prayer, meditation, church attendance/fellowship, etc.
- Do not begin projects that you cannot complete satisfactorily.
- Do not over obligate
- Pace yourself to allow an even flow of demands.
- Have a daily schedule and "to do" list to help you stay organized.
- Set reasonable boundaries for yourself.
- Learn to recognize the physical signs of stress and the behaviors associated with your reaction to things that happen in ordinary life situations.

Tools to Assist Your Troops

Group Debrief/Support:

Not enough can be said for the therapeutic values of group discussions about a common experience. By re-visiting and discovering core issues surrounding common experiences veterans of the Vietnam War were the first to find the importance of "talking it out" in rap groups. Robert Jay Lifton, a psychiatrist and researcher internationally known for his work with survivors of the atomic bomb at Hiroshima and victims of the Nazi holocaust, says, "It is important to emphasize that the veterans themselves initiated the groups." However, over the years it has been found that group therapy led by a mental health professional (or clergy) is more effective because they understand the emotionally impacting issues that arise. They also offer educational direction to provide for positive life changes. However, as a military leader, you should be prepared to facilitate a group within your unit in times of crisis.

Clearly, the issues and events of war deepen with isolation and silence, therefore it is very important to provide a forum for engaged troops to "air" things out. Group processing provides healing and restoration of inner peace through a common focus and trust.

Group Structure:

As the group members convene for the first meeting it is important to create "ground rules" that everyone can agree on. It is the first step in building an honest community,* and if these rules are *not* agreed upon by everyone involved it cannot exist. If particular person fails to agree to the ground rules of the group this might be an indication that they do not want to be a member. Keep it voluntary. (*A community in this sense is the gathering of people coming together to accept each other and work out issues for a better life. When greater trust, sensitivity, acceptance, intimacy, and better communication skills are developed, and practiced, there is a foundation for community. M. Scott Peck—The Different Drum—Simon and Schuster - 1987)

An example** of these group rules are:

- Each member attends on their own volition (this cannot be mandatory), and they reserve the choice to discontinue at anytime. (It is the facilitator's responsibility to follow-up with any group member who decides to leave.)
- Confidentiality is critical. What is shared in the group stays in the group, although lessons learned are sometimes important to share with loved ones and significant outside parties, but identities should never be disclosed.

- Everyone must be on time. Late comers break the flow and dilutes the trust of the group.
- One person speaks at a time. Respect each other's communication.
- No "grandstanding". Pet issues (political, religious, etc.) to sway others' opinions are not allowed.
- Every member commits to strive for self-improvement.
- If unable to attend group, members obligate to notify the leader.
- No alcohol or substance use prior to the meeting.
- The leader must explain to the members that their anger is normal, but no violence will be tolerated as this puts other group members at risk.
- If anger emerges there must be a preplanned arrangement in place that the leader implements at his discretion. (Cooling off period, take a 15 minute walk, etc.)

**These are only sample rules that have been successfully used before. They can be modified to suit the make-up of each particular group.*

The Group Meeting:

Who facilitates? To create the safest environment possible, and to ensure freedom of expression, the confidentiality of a chaplain or chaplaincy staff member is the preferred facilitator for these group meetings.

Below is a sample blueprint for a successful group meeting.

Check-In:

At the beginning of the meeting each member is given an opportunity to check in with the group. (A short and concise description of how you are presently feeling.) This is merely a *check-in* and not a time to go into long, drawn out explanations, complaints, etc. That can come later after everyone has had a chance to check-in. The facilitator can begin the group with one person and goes through steps such as these:

- How are you feeling? (What was your best experience last week?) (What was your worst?)
- What good coping have you done since the last group meeting?
- Any self-medication (drugs or alcohol)
- What unsafe behavior have you participated in? (i.e. high risk activities)
- How are your military experiences impinging on your present life circumstances?
- What commitment can you make today that will help you work through the negative impact of your experiences? (i.e. "I will replace negative thoughts with positive thoughts as often as possible.")

Check-Out:

At the end of each session, the facilitator once again gives members an opportunity to sum up their session.

- Name one thing you got out of today's group session. What is your closing feeling?
- What is your new commitment to work on before the next session?
- Declare what positive action you will take if you have a problem before the next group session. (i.e. "I will call or talk with _____ to process the experience.")

Core Concepts to Focus on in the Group:
- Stay safe
- Respect yourself and others
- Use positive coping—not substances—to escape pain
- Make the present and future better than the past
- Learn to trust
- Take care of your body
- Get help from safe people
- Never, never, never give up.
- Freely exchange contact information with one another and encourager

PROLOGUE

❦

A View of the
Combat Community

THE TRANSITION FROM CIVILIAN LIFE
to military life contrasts like night and day. The first thing new
civilians-to-soldiers give up is their freedom. They lose much of
their self determination by having to submit to commanding
authority, and are required to fall in line with a myriad of other
components within a giant machine where individuality is not a
part of the equation. In order to adapt to the military and its
unfamiliar conditions, young soldiers must find within themselves a mechanism to help adjust and cope with the challenges of
this new environment. That mechanism, or tool, gives us conso-
lation of surviving through a "community" with others to whom
fate has brought together.

During a time of war, however, new and more demanding
transitions are added to these trials. The danger of being
wounded or killed is clear and tangible, and becomes a constant
burden on the emotional state. The switch from a life of peace
and security to the conditions of war cause further unrest. These
conditions add even more weight to the emotional burden of each
soldier.

Conversely, the soldier having formed bonds with his comrades now feels solidarity with them. Unit pride and honor all

play a part in this dynamic, but the responsibility for survival of self, and the welfare of those he is fighting with, contributes most to a soldier's motivation to continue in the fight.

When one spends months or years with fellow combatants engaging in wartime activities we inherently become part of a working community. Not merely a "group", but a community made up of tried and true partners of survival who have the best interests of the other members in mind. (A "group" can merely be a number of people who congregate and never get to know each other. It does not require affiliation…but participating in a community does.) Military relationships are unique because they demand a sense of community with everyone involved. They do so from the most basic human need—the need to survive.

One of the most painful aspects of coming home from war (and back to civilian life) is leaving the units in which we served. These communities you were forced to carve out for yourself with blood, sweat and tears, now have to be abruptly abandoned. As you leave you reflect. It becomes obvious how each member has changed within themselves during the time spent together. You passed each test and endured according to the demands placed upon each of you, both as an individual and participant of a true community.

As a team you learned how to live through extraordinary hardships, and you cared that everyone made it through. You passed around the same soggy, rain-soaked cigarettes from man to man and no one was left out. Together you learned to tolerate MREs (meals-ready-to-eat) and C-rations. You were satisfied with snuggling up and sleeping in the driest part of a foxhole — and perhaps even in the arms of someone who had been a perfect stranger only days before.

In the most primal ways you came to know another soldier's character. You did this through shared hardships of the gravest of natures. And, in the middle of it all you witnessed another human's weaknesses and amazing strengths as you worked to overcome the rigors and horrors of war.

No matter how bad the conditions were, or how often you dreamed of coming home to a normal life, leaving our close knit, powerful, and intimate community was very difficult. What you had just seen and done with your comrades for those many long months could never be replaced in one's heart. When you leave it, it is like a tearing in your soul. This "community" is what veterans long for when they get home and sadly, many never find it again. I believe if community can be re-established in civilian life, then many of the prevailing re-adjustment problems would dissipate. Relationships are at the heartbeat of community, and vice versa.

Resolving Conflicts— The Work of Community

During my time on active duty in the U. S. Army, I received no instruction on how to negotiate a peaceful resolution with anyone...especially those considered to be my enemies. In war, our primary objective was to close with the enemy and eliminate him. When we could not neutralize or overcome the enemy, we would pull back or retreat. From the time mankind began strategizing and making war, this has been the military way. It is still part of the modern military mentality.

Fight or flight—live or die—win or lose. When we returned to civilian life many of us did not let go of our old ways of thinking. At times when situations become intense, some of us resort to what we know best...fight like hell or run the other direction. This behavior is not conducive to making good lasting relationships in a civilian world. Ex-combatants must create another type of community or fail socially.

With relationship building, we must not avoid conflicts, but rather seek to resolve them. This is easier said than done because we were never trained on that part of the drill. By learning the right way to resolve conflicts, we do great justice to well-grounded relationships. When conflicts are successfully resolved, we come away feeling like a team that has tackled, and overcome an adversary together. As a result, we become stronger in mind, body, and spirit...a unified front.

Veterans, especially those who have been exposed to combat, need to be encouraged and reaffirmed. Though our patterns are firmly entrenched, it's never too late to do better in relationships.

We can change! We can choose to learn new skills in resolving conflicts, and when we do, we make the days ahead more productive and loving for everyone involved. Without being too simplistic, it is really just a simple matter of making a choice. Either we can ignore our worsening situation with the people around us, or we can forge new paths toward middle ground. As we do, we will go far in developing and sustaining good healthy relationships to pave the way for a precious peace in the communities in which we now live.

Chuck Dean

Preparing Families for the Homecoming

IN THIS SECTION WE HAVE INCLUDED A short course to help family members and loved ones prepare for the eventual return of those serving in a war zone.

Hearts on the Homefront
Phase #1 of "Turning Your Heart Toward Home"
Workbook Course
A Publication of:
Hearts Toward Home International
1050 Larrabee Avenue
Suite 104, PMB 714
Bellingham, Washington 98225-7367
(360) 714-1525
www.heartstowardhome.com
Published by WordSmith Books, LLC, P.O. Box 68065, Seattle, WA. 98168

Course Instructions
This course is designed for group settings. However, it can be studied and applied individually. Keep in mind that a large percentage of the benefits of group interaction may be lost.

A facilitator will convene the meetings and the course should take approximately 3-4 hours. If the group chooses to do it in multiple meetings, then it can be done at the pace that is convenient for everyone involved.

At the conclusion of the course you will find an "After Action Form". By filling this out we will be able to do such things as improve the course, keep participants connected, and update each person on other materials and courses that are available to assist military and veteran families.

Reference suggestions:

The following are some books that we recommend. We believe they will help in the process. Each book has a website from where they can be ordered.

"Down Range: To Iraq and Back" Bridget C. Cantrell, Ph.D. and Chuck Dean
www.heartstowardhome.com (Pre-publication orders are available. Release in Spring/summer of 2005).

"When the War is Over: A New One Begins" Chuck Dean and Bette Nordberg
www.namvetbook.com

"Heroes at Home: Help and Hope for America's Military Families" Ellie Kay
www.bethanyhouse.com

"Solo Ops: A Survival Guide for Military Wives" Hilary Martin
Orders@Xlibris.com

"Surviving Deployment: A Guide for Military Families" Karen Pavlicin www.amazon.com

Introduction

The purpose of this short informational course is to serve as a preliminary study to the more detailed "Turning Your Heart Toward Home" workbook course by Bridget C. Cantrell, Ph.D. with Chuck Dean. That course is intended to help troops (and loved ones) re-integrate *after* returning from serving in military hazard zones for extended periods of time. *However, this preparatory course is designed (and very beneficial) solely for those on the homefront while their loved one is deployed.* It is a phase #1 course that should precede the primary workbook course.

In our research we have found it necessary, and of great importance, to help those folks waiting on the homefront become more aware of what to expect upon their serviceperson's return.

Hopefully this material will eliminate the many surprises, misunderstandings, and heartaches that may come along the way.

[We have compiled certain lists of examples, traits, habits and stressors within this course. However, these are not exhaustive lists and most certainly can be added to throughout the journey.]

Each troop *knows*, that they will be challenged in re-adjusting upon their return. The better equipped we are at home to work with them will make all the difference in how well that re-adjustment goes. A case in point is the following excerpt in a recent e-mail from the war zone:

> *"I sit here today a man at a crossroad. After almost 15 months of military service that took me from the Pacific Northwest halfway around the world to the Middle East, I prepare myself to re-enter the world that I know and truly love. The world I know is marked by the gentle voice of my daughter urging me to come and play with her; my wife holding me when I wake in the morning; and the time I shall soon devote to getting to know my son who just turned 2. It is a transition that troubles me..."*

Welcome to the course. We hope the information will be valuable in the home coming you are waiting for.

Section One:
How will it be Different?

It is impossible to say exactly how your loved will be when they return. Everyone has a different resiliency and toleration level to hardships. We can, however, give you a combination of signs along the trail, "red-flag" warnings, and some actual experiences from veterans of earlier wars.

Change: Listed below are some ways that we have seen returnees change because of the exposure to the hardships and dangers of war. (Remember, some of these changes may seem unreal or trite to you, but if your loved one is reacting to them—they are an issue to be recognized and dealt with.) As a group, discuss what possible methods you can plan in order to cope with each change in a productive way. Brainstorming with people who find themselves in similar situations such as yours is an extremely important component to coping and healing.

The service person:

- Is now quiet and over-reflective (almost as if they are not present).
- Is now nervous and jumpy at the slightest provocation.
- Is now overly sensitive to sights, sounds, and situations that are reminders of the war zone.
- Is now short-tempered and becomes easily frustrated or angry over seemingly small matters.
- Cannot tolerate simple mistakes made by those around him or her.
- Cannot remain in crowds or social gatherings for any length of time. Is always looking for a way out.

Quirks/habits: Your loved one may have developed some quirks or habits as a means to physically survive or to take care of themselves emotionally while in the war zone. As a group, discuss what possible methods you can plan in order to cope with this list of possibilities in a productive way.

The service person:

- May have a "defensive "perimeter wire" in place and cannot allow anyone to get too close to them. (This could be a result of subconscious vows not to allow anyone too close because it is too painful when you lose them.)
- Sleeping with the lights on all night.
- Sleeping with weapons.
- Sitting in "strategic" places in public places to detect and be alert for sudden enemy attacks.
- May not want to unpack the clothes they brought back from the war zone. (Too many reminders are in the duffle bag, or they may have the feeling they will be called back and need to have things packed.)

Section Two:
What Can I do to Prepare?

The very first thing you need to do is prepare yourself mentally for the changes and differences that will prevail for a while in your relationship. As much as we all want things to go back to the way they were *before* deployment, realize this is an unreal expectation. To think that you and your loved can go back to square one and pick up where you left off is setting yourself up for a loss. Time has passed and lives have changed. Be progressive and stay focused in the here and now. Here are some ways to prepare. Discuss them as a group and list out productive coping methods.

- For marriage partners: Plan to start the dating process all over again. Rekindle the friendship and romantic aspects of your relationship, and sort out the responsibilities afterwards.
- For family members: Plan to view the relationship in the present and avoid trying to re-live childhood activities, remembrances, and/or dreams. (After engaging in wartime activities, dreams and innocent notions of life may have been shattered and most likely the furthest thing from their mind. Bringing the memories of their past life can remind them too much of what they have lost.)

Plan ways to be sensitive to your loved one's idiosyncrasies. For example, it is considerate to ask them where *they* would like to sit in a restaurant. Refrain from demanding that they go shopping in crowded malls. Do what you can to keep the kids from crawling on them too much (remember the "perimeter wire"?). Do not take it personal if your loved one does not hug as much as you would like. If you give them space by understanding and respecting the "wire" principle, hopefully they will draw closer in time.

Section Three:
Exactly what is Post-Traumatic Stress?

Since the Vietnam War, a growing body of information has been gathered on the effects trauma. What was previously called "soldier's heart", "shell shock" or "battle fatigue" in previous wars, has been referred to as Post-traumatic stress disorder (PTSD) since 1985. Some common manifestations are intrusive thoughts, flashbacks, hyper-arousal, anxiety, reactions triggered by loud noises, nightmares, emotionally numb (or over-reactive), unexplained anger/rage, and depression are just some of its major symptoms.

With the terror of September 11, 2001 still fresh in our national psyche, millions have become aware of the reactions to trauma firsthand as their eyes were fixed on the television sets and collectively experienced "9/11". As we have seen by this, PTSD is not limited to combat on the battlefield. These same symptoms are even familiar to many survivors of family abuse—emotional, physical and sexual.

Stress is a normal and personal response that our bodies and minds have in order to meet the demands that different situations present to us. When we contend with these demands and it goes beyond the range of normal human experiences (and war trauma is certainly something beyond that range), then we are likely to become more vulnerable to incurring the severe symptoms of "post" traumatic stress (PTSD).

Is PTSD a Mental Illness?

It is important to note that PTSD is *not* a mental illness. It is a normal reaction to an abnormal set of circumstances. What your loved one endured during war has gone beyond the realm of usual or routine human experiences. PTSD, therefore, is a reaction to the extreme stress people encounter during threats of danger to themselves or others and/or the fear of death. The level of stress resulting from this fear or danger may hinder those who suffer with PTSD in adjusting to civilian (or normal) life after the experience(s).

How long does PTSD last?

This is a common question. The objective with treating PTSD is to develop coping skills and awareness of how a person is triggered (A "trigger" is a reminder in one's environment which activates: anxiety, fear, flashbacks, anger, nausea, hyper-alertness in addition to other symptoms of PTSD). There is no evidence that

PTSD will ever be completely eradicated from a person's life. However, there is an abundance of information, which supports the importance of positive interventions and treatments for the successful management of the various symptoms associated with PTSD. Once a person has been traumatized to this degree there may be ongoing episodes and manifestations of PTSD throughout their lifetime. The good news is that in many cases it can be managed by simply being aware and knowledgeable of the various symptoms and triggers. Educating those concerned about PTSD, and practicing self-care, are the two key safeguards that will help make the process smoother.

How Can I Help?

For the partner or family member living with a person with PTSD, it is important for them to be supportive. You can actually be a "second set of eyes" by heightening your awareness and increasing your empathy, so that you can understand how your loved one is being affected by the symptoms of PTSD. Being aware of your partner's triggers is important to building trust and intimacy in the relationship. It is important for a person with PTSD to feel supported and loved. The chances of this happening are better if the partner or family member understands, and is involved with them on their journey towards healing.

As a group, please discuss what possible methods you can plan in order to cope with the following possible PTSD symptoms.

Major PTSD Symptoms to Become Acquainted With:
- Depression
- Cynicism and distrust of government and authority
- Anger
- Alienation
- Isolation
- Sleep disturbances
- Poor concentration
- Tendency to react under stress with survival tactics
- Psychic or emotional numbing
- Negative self-image

- Memory impairment
- Emotional constriction
- Hypersensitivity to justice
- Loss of interest in work and activities
- Problems with intimate relationships
- Survivor guilt
- Difficulty with authority figures
- Hyper-alertness—hyper arousal
- Avoidance of activities that arouse memories of traumas in war zone
- Emotional distance from children, wife, and others
- Self-deceiving and self-punishing patterns of behavior, such as an inability to talk about war experiences, fear of losing others, and a tendency to fits of rage
- Suicidal feelings and thoughts
- Flashbacks to dangers and combat
- Fantasies of retaliation and destruction
- High risk employment/recreation

Section Four:
How Can I Prepare My Children?

Children will have understandable fears for the safety of parents sent overseas. Therefore, it is important for you, the parent or family member, to know what to expect in children while their loved one is deployed. You can prepare the child first and foremost by educating yourself on spotting and dealing with their potential reactions to the new experience. It is crucial to provide opportunity for children to discuss their concerns and to help them separate real from imagined fears. It is also important to limit exposure to media coverage of violence.

Parents and relatives at home can help by letting children honestly express feelings and concerns. Frequent telephone calls, letters and/or email are essential in helping children feel connected to, and loved by, absent parents. Because repeated scenes of destruction of lives and property are featured in the daily news media, they may understand that "enemies of the United States" can harm their loved one. We adults need to help children feel encouraged and safe at a time when the world seems to be a more dangerous place. As much as possible we need to carry their share of the worry and pain that war causes. It is our duty.

I was once standing in an art display of very graphic Vietnam War scenes when a young mother came through leading a small boy of perhaps 4 years old. She was curious and wanted to take in what she could without spending a lot of time exposing her son to the impacting scenes. As she hastily dragged the boy along, he suddenly pointed at one of the paintings and asked, "Momma, what is that?" What she said next remains with me as most profound. She wisely answered him, "Someday you'll know, but for now I'll carry that load so you won't have to." She hurriedly exited the display and went about being a protective mom.

Emotional Responses

Emotional responses vary in nature and severity from child to child.   Nonetheless, there are some similarities in how children feel when their lives are impacted by war or the threat of war:

Fear: Fear may be the predominant reaction—fear for the safety of those in the military. When children hear rumors at school and pick up bits of information from television their imaginations may run wild. They may think the worst, however unrealistic it may be.

Loss of control: Military actions are something over which children—and most adults—have no control. Lack of control can be overwhelming and confusing. Children may grasp at any control that they have, including refusing to cooperate, go to school, part with favorite toys, or leave your side.

Anger: Anger is a common reaction and may often be a substitute (or familiar emotion) to express sadness or loss.   Unfortunately, anger is often expressed at those to whom children are closest. Children may direct anger toward classmates and neighbors because they cannot express their anger toward those responsible for their parents being sent to war. Some children may show unexpected anger toward parents who are at home or those in the military; even to the extent that they do not want to write letters or draw pictures or send gifts. (This could be the child's way of developing their own "perimeter wire".)

Loss of stability: War or military deployment interrupts routines. It is unsettling. Children can feel insecure when their usual schedules and activities are disrupted, which increases their level of stress and need for reassurance. Even the adults are dealing with their own instability, and children are easily influence by their environment. It is important to use good judgment in your daily behavior.

Isolation: Children who have a family member in the military, but who do not live near a military base, may feel more isolated. Children of reserve members called to active duty may not know others in the same situation. Such children may feel resentment and sadness toward friends whose families are intact (not deployed). They may strike out at signs of normalcy around them. Another group of children who may feel isolated are dependents of military families who have accompanied a remaining parent back to a hometown, or who are staying with relatives while both parents are gone. Not only do these children experience separation from parents, but they also experience the loss of familiar faces and surroundings.

Confusion: This can occur on two levels. First, children may feel confused about the concept of war and what further dangers might arise. Second, children may have trouble understanding the difference between violence as entertainment and the real events taking place on the news. Today's children live in the world of *Armageddon, Independence Day, Air Force One,* and cartoon Super Heroes. Some of the modern media violence is unnervingly real. Youngsters may have difficulty separating reality from fantasy, cartoon heroes, and villains, from the government soldiers and real terrorists. Separating the realities of war from media fantasy does require adult help.

What Can Parents Do?

Everyone, including adults, feels stressed during times of crisis and uncertainty. If your children seem to need help beyond what is normally available at home or school, seek mental health services in your community. Psychologists, counselors and social workers can identify appropriate services and help with the referral process. For most children, adults can provide adequate support by the following actions:

Acknowledge Children's Feelings:

Knowing what to say is often difficult. When no other words come to mind, a hug and saying "This is really hard for you/us" will help, but giving them an avenue of positive re-direction by engaging them in a stimulating activity will do wonders.

Try to recognize the feelings underlying children's actions and put them into words. Say something like, "I can see you have feelings about this. Tell me more about them." Be careful not tell your children how *they* are feeling, instead let them tell you. A very good technique to express emotion is through art, music, and acting. Invite the child to use these methods to physically demonstrate their feelings. (Younger children may find that using these alternative modes of communication are easier ways to express themselves.)

Sometimes children may voice concern about what will happen to them if a parent does not return. If this occurs, offer something like this, "You will be well taken care of. You won't be alone. What would this look like to you if this happened? Let me tell you our plan and we can work together."

At times when your children are most upset, do not deny the seriousness of the situation. Saying to children, "Don't cry, everything will be okay," does not reflect how the child feels and does not make them feel better. Nevertheless, do not forget to express hope and faith that things will be okay; remembering to be truthful with what is appropriate for the age and situation. Determine as to whether or not your own fears are being projected onto your child. It is not appropriate for your child to carry your burden as well as their own.

Older children, in particular, may require help clarifying what they believe about war and the role of the United States in this current conflict. They may ask some very poignant questions which you need to be prepared to address, such as, "Will my parent kill someone?" and "Are we killing innocent people in other countries?" are issues which may need discussion. It may be a time to speak to a clergy person and discuss the morality of war. Perhaps it is also good to remind the children that we hope our military can do enough to stop the war and help bring peace in other countries.

Always be honest with children. Share your fears and concerns with discretion, while at the same time reassuring them that responsible adults are in charge.

If participation in a faith community is part of your family life, talk to your faith leader about how to help your child think about the concepts of death and killing, in age-appropriate terms. This can be very important to calming your fear, as well as those of your children.

Try to maintain normal routines and schedules to provide a sense of stability and security within the family, school and your community.

Help children maintain a sense of control by taking some action:

Send letters, cookies or magazines to those in the military.

Help older children find a family who has a parent on active duty and arrange some volunteer babysitting times for that family or offer to provide meals occasionally. These types of activities and support are vital for feeling a sense of purpose and community that can serve as healthy and productive expressions of compassion.

If a family member is away, make plans for some special activities:

Gatherings with other families who have a loved one on active duty can help provide support for you as well as for your children.

Special parent and child times can provide an extra sense of security, which might be needed. Let your child know that you will set aside a particular half hour each day to play. Make the time as pleasant and child-centered as possible. Return phone calls later and make your child the real focus of that special time.

Organize a consistent pattern, which ensures a child of positive expectations, such as regular meal times. Morning and bedtime rituals (bathing, prayer, reading stories, etc.) can provide a wonderful sense of peace and security for both parent and child.

Involve children in planning how to cope. Control and ownership are fostered when children help to plan strategies for dealing with a situation. Children often have practical and creative ideas for coping. Be open and willing to adjust your life accordingly. Be flexible without losing a sense of control.

Expect and respond to changes in behavior:

All children will likely display some signs of stress. Some immature, aggressive, oppositional, as well as regressive, withdrawn and isolative behaviors are reactions to the uncertainty of this situation. We advise that you seek professional help if these behaviors continue. Just by having an objective third party to intervene can make a big difference in the well-being of your child's mental health.

Even though there is a significant shift the family structure it is important to maintain consistent expectations for behavior. Be sure children understand that the same rules apply that were in place prior to the change.

It is important that the roles remain intact. You do not want to undermine this principle by imposing a false authority upon a child. For example, one of the most damaging expectations, or "assignments", is to say, "Your dad is gone to war, so now you're the man of the house." This does not work. It confuses the child who may now see this status as an added obligation and burden to uphold.

Some children whose parents are on active duty may have difficulty at bedtime. Maintain a regular bedtime routine. Be flexible about nightlights, siblings sharing a room, sleeping with special toys, and sitting with your child as they fall asleep. Doing so typically does not cause life-long habits. These are comforting means to provide reassurance to a child.

Extra support, consistency, empathy and patience will help children return to routines and their more usual behavior patterns. If children show extreme reactions (aggression, withdrawal, sleeping problems, etc.), consult with a mental health professional regarding the symptoms of severe stress disorders, and the possible need for a referral to a mental health agency.

Keep adult issues from overwhelming children:

Do not let your children focus too much of their time and energy on the situation of having a loved one at war. If children are choosing to watch the news for hours each evening, find other activities for them. You may also need to watch the news less intensely and spend more time in alternative family activities.

Know the facts about developments in the war. Be prepared to answer your children's questions factually, and take time to think about how you want to frame events and your reactions to them.

Try not to let financial strains be a major concern of children. For National Guard or Reserve families going from a civilian job to active duty in the military may cut family income. Children are not capable of dealing with this issue on an ongoing basis. Telling a child that you need to be more careful with spending is appropriate, but be cautious about placing major burdens on them.

And finally…self-care. Take time for yourself and try to deal with your own reactions to the situation as fully as possible. This, too, will help your child's well-being.

Section Five:
Self-Care

When the oxygen mask drops out of the ceiling on airplanes, adults are instructed to place their masks on themselves before doing the same for any small children near them. It takes no explanation to see why this sequence is vital to survival. Likewise, it is a perfect illustration of why your *self-care* is so important. If you are not taking care of yourself properly, it is unlikely that your family will get the best care from you either. Only when we first help ourselves can we effectively help others. Caring for yourself

is one of the most important—and one of the most often forgotten—things you can do as a parent who is carrying the load while
a loved one is deployed. When *your* needs are taken care of, the
person you care for will benefit as well.

When it comes to surviving the deployment of a loved one,
you must do what you can to nurture yourself both physically and
emotionally. This can be a difficult task since you are now standing in for both sides of the parenting spectrum, and have many
more responsibilities to tend to than before.

In this section we will offer some tips and guidelines for you
to focus upon which will help you in this self-care procedure.
These are only a few of the things you can do to put special attention on yourself. Use this course time to discuss and share different methods of self-care with the group. You most likely will
discover many more useful ideas from the others. Take good notes
as the group shares.

Tips for Self-Care:
- Learn and use stress-reduction techniques. (Relaxation, deep
  breathing, etc.).
- Attend to your own healthcare needs and implement a vita-
  min program.
- Get proper rest and nutrition.
- Exercise regularly.
- Take time off without feeling guilty.
- Participate in pleasant, nurturing activities with other grown-
  ups.
- Seek and accept the support of others. Spend time each day
  conversing (in person, phone, or e-mail) with another sup-
  portive adult who can share your burden.
- Seek supportive counseling when you need it, or talk to a
  trusted counselor or friend.
- Identify and acknowledge your feelings.
- Change the negative ways you view situations.
- Take up a personal hobby.
- Limit your exposure and use of alcohol and drugs.
- Set goals. (Take baby steps).

Conclusion

We hope that this small course has helped in your journey to survive deployment. It is our hope that you will consider attending our more in-depth course "Turning Your Heart Toward Home". This subsequent course is conducted jointly with you and your service person upon their return. Please indicate your interest in participating in this important course. Please take a moment to fill out this form and pass it on to your course facilitator.

After Action Form

Name _____

Partner or family member's name_____

Branch of service _____

Present military unit _____

Address_____ Zip_____

Phone_____

E-mail _____

Was this course satisfactory to you?   Yes   No

If "no" can you explain?   _____

_____

_____

How can it be improved? _____

_____

Would you recommend it to others?   Yes   No

If "no" can you explain?_____

_____

Do you plan to attend the "Turning Your Heart Toward Home" course when your loved one returns from overseas?   Yes   No

May we send you updates and reminders through the mail?
Yes   No

Please feel free to contact the authors about any part of this course or questions that you may have regarding deployment or re-integration.

Hearts Toward Home International
1050 Larrabee Avenue
Suite 104, PMB 714
Bellingham, Washington 98225-7367
(360) 714-1525 www.heartstowardhome.com

Resources

Hearts Toward Home International is an organization formed for the purpose of providing support, counseling, training, educational classes, books, materials, as well as re-integration and re-adjustment workshop/forums for military personnel (both active duty and veterans) and their families. This corporation also trains facilitators and counselors in the skills of re-integrating military personnel with loved ones and the civilian environs to which they return. The specific use of *"Turning Your Heart Toward Home"* workbook course is emphasized.

www.heartstowardhome.com
Bridget C. Cantrell, Ph.D.
1050 Larrabee Avenue
Suite 104, PMB 714
Bellingham, Washington 98225-7367
(360) 714-1525

Military OneSource was established in June 2004 as a one-stop shop for all service members who need "help to cope with life's little—and not so little—issues." The service, which was previously broken down by individual service branch, offers 24-hour help by phone (800-342-9647) or by e-mail. Its web site provides advice on everything from coping with stress to caring for an elderly relative to recovering from drug and alcohol addiction. In addition to online articles, there are booklets, CDs, audiotapes, and interactive tools available, all free.

ARMY—"Army OneSource" 800-464-8107
MARINES—"Marines OneSource" 800-869-0278
NAVY—"Navy OneSource" 800-540-4123
AIR FORCE—"Air Force OneSource" 800-707-5784

National Suicide Prevention Lifeline
(800-273-TALK-8255)
The only national suicide intervention hotline funded by the federal government, this number works 24 hours, seven days a week and is comprised of over 100 crisis centers nationwide.

The National Center for Post-Traumatic Stress Disorder
http://www.ncptsd.org/
Just about everything you might ever want to know about PTSD — from the biology of the disease to its impact on spirituality — is provided on this Web site in the form of fact sheets, medical papers, videos and more. The NCPTSD is a part of the VA that works to advance the clinical care and social welfare of America's veterans through research, education, and training in the science, diagnosis, and treatment of PTSD and stress-related disorders.

VA Facilities & Locator Directory
http://www1.va.gov/directory/guide/home.asp?isFlash=1

Social Security Office Locator
1-800-772-1213 - SOCIAL SECURITY BENEFITS
Veterans with PTSD may be able to obtain Social Security benefits, even if the VA refuses them veterans' benefits. The Social Security Administration (SSA) offers both disability insurance (SSDI) and supplemental security income (SSI) benefits. Veterans can receive both SSDI and VA disability compensation without an offset. Unlike VA compensation benefits that are measured in degrees of disability, SSA benefits require a total disability that will last at least one year.

Vietnam Veterans of America (VVA) PTSD Claims Guide (Designed to assist all veterans)
http://www.vva.org/benefits/ptsd.htm
The purpose of this guide is to assist the veteran, or the veteran's survivor(s), in presenting a claim for benefits based on exposure to psychologically traumatic events during military service that has resulted in post-traumatic stress disorder (PTSD).

Deployment LINK
1-800 497 6261

Deployment Health Support
Four Skyline Place
5113 Leesburg Pike, Suite 901
Falls Church, VA 22041
http://deploymentlink.osd.mil/deploy/post_deploy/post_deploy_
intro.shtml
The difficulty of readjusting to home is addressed on this Web
site, with input from all four branches of the services, the
Reserves and the VA.

VA Readjustment Counseling Services http://www.va.gov/rcs/
You will be able to locate a Vet Center in your state on this Web site.
Vet Centers are small community organizations managed by the
VA and dedicated to providing counseling for combat veterans
from combat veterans. The site also links to tele-health services
and the National Center for PTSD.

REALifelines
http://www.dol.gov/vets/programs/Real-life/main.htm
1-877-US2-JOBS/872-5627
The Recovery and Employment Assistance Lifelines initiative is a
joint project of the U.S. Department of Labor, the Bethesda
Naval Medical Center and the Walter Reed Army Medical
Center. It works to create a seamless, personalized assistance network to ensure that seriously wounded and injured service
members who cannot return to active duty are trained for
rewarding new careers in the private sector.

National Veterans Foundation
http://www.nvf.org/
The only nationwide non-governmental national hotline for veterans and their families providing crisis intervention, resource
referral, benefits information and emotional support: 800-777-
4443. (Monday-Friday, 9 am to 5 pm).

National Gulf War Resource Center
http://www.ngwrc.org/
Steve Robinson
Executive Director
National Gulf War Resource Center, Inc.
8605 Cameron Street Suite 400
Silver Spring, MD 20910
301-585-4000 x162
This is an international coalition of organizations that has been advocating for veterans since 1995 and is run by former Army Ranger Steve Robinson. The NGWRC is a resource for information, support, referrals and how to file claims. Under "Resources" there is a self-help guide on PTSD, and be sure to explore the "PTSD and Readjustment" bulletin board.

PTSD Alliance
http://www.ptsdalliance.org/home2.html
(877) 507-PTSD
PTSD Alliance was launched in 2000 and works with anyone suffering from Post Traumatic Stress, including military veterans. The Alliance is a multi-disciplinary group of professional and advocacy organizations that have joined forces to provide educational resources to medical and health care professionals, individuals diagnosed with PTSD and their loved ones, the general public and the media.

Employer Support of the Guard and Reserve (ESGR)
http://www.esgr.org/
1-800-336-4590
Guardsmen and Reservists have the right to return to their civilian jobs following their service. Those who think their employers have acted unfairly—for instance, if they believe they were fired because of their military service—should contact the ESGR.

National Organization of Veterans Advocates (NOVA)
1-800-810-8387
This is an organization of attorneys who regularly practice before the Court of Appeals for Veterans Claims (which has jurisdiction over Board of Veterans Affairs decisions).   Its members are available to represent you at the Court. For a list of these attorneys contact: the National Organization of Veterans' Advocates (NOVA) at (800) 810-8387. If no private practitioners are willing to represent you at the Court, it might be possible to obtain pro bono representation through the Veterans Pro Bono Consortium. The Court will send you information about this opportunity if you file an appeal there.

National Military Family Association (NMFA)
http://www.nmfa.org/site/PageServer
1.800.260.0218
The NMFA's mission is to provide timely and useful information to military families. There is much to explore on this organization's Web site.

Point Man International
1-800-877-VETS
http://www.geocities.com/~pointmen/
This organization is a veterans-for-veterans support organization that provides spiritual support for veterans and their families. Weekly support groups are available nationwide.

Women Organizing Women (WOW) Group - Veteran Advocacy.
Susan Avila-Smith established the "Women Organizing Women" WOW group in 1997. Monthly meetings at the Seattle VAMC, and American Lake in Lakewood, Washington with forums used to provide advocacy and network vital information regarding services and benefits to women veterans and their providers.
www.Wowvet.com
smith715@comcast.net
(425) 313-7666
(206) 783-8005

Tips Regarding Veterans Claims

When to Apply: You should notify the VA of the benefits you want at the earliest possible time. From anywhere in the U.S., you can call the nearest VA Regional Office (VARO) by using the following number: 1-800-827-1000. Do not wait until you have gathered all of the evidence that you think you will need. Every day you delay can mean another day of benefits lost forever.
Warning: Do not be discouraged by a VA employee who says you are not entitled to benefits. Put your claim in writing and insist on a written reply from the VA.

How to Apply: To apply, send the VA a letter stating that you have a problem with your nerves, emotions, etc., that arose out of your military service. This is called an informal claim and will count as an application (although you will eventually be required to submit a formal application on VA form 21-526). If you have not heard from the VA within one month, you should call to confirm that your application has been received. If you have applied before, been denied and did not file a formal appeal, send a letter that states that you wish to reopen your claim with new and material evidence.

What to Apply For: The VA offers monetary benefits to veterans with service-connected disabilities (under its disability compensation program) and to veterans with serious non-service-connected disabilities (under its pension program). Survivors may be entitled to benefits if the VA determines that the veteran had a service-connected disability that caused, or substantially contributed to cause, the veteran's death. (See below).

Who Can Apply: A claim for PTSD is not limited to veterans who participated in combat with the enemy. For example, sexual assaults, vehicular accidents, being a victim of a crime or other sufficiently traumatic events during service can support a diagnosis of PTSD for VA claims purposes. Merely being in stressful situations, or being "stressed-out" generally will not be sufficient.

Survivors: Sometimes a veteran's survivor, including spouses, children and dependent parents can apply for service-connected death benefits (Dependency and Indemnity Compensation or DIC program) or for the non service-connected death benefits (pension program). A survivor might be able to show that a veteran with service-connected PTSD died as a consequence of a disease that was secondary to PTSD, e.g., cardiovascular disease, substance abuse (in certain cases).

WARNING: If you have applied in the past and were denied, you may have a hard time re-opening your claim. There is no specific VA application form to use to re-open your claim, but there are specific rules you must follow in terms of the evidence required in order for the VA to reopen the claim. Consult your service representative for details on what kind of "new and material evidence" you need to present.

(This information was provided by various contributors and has not been verified by the authors for accuracy.)

References

American Psychiatric Association. *Diagnostic and Statistical Manual of Mental Disorders.* 4th ed.-TR. Washington, D.C.: American Psychiatric Association, 2000.

Brende, Joel, (1989). Publication of Trauma Recovery Center, Augusta, GA.

Bureau of Justice Statistics Special Report Veterans in Prison or Jail, (January 2000).

Cantrell, Bridget C., (1999). *Social Support as a Function of Post Traumatic Stress Disorder (PTSD) within Washington State Vietnam Veteran Populations.* (Doctoral Dissertation, Pacific Graduate School of Psychology, 1999) UMI Number: 9944407.

Fleming-Michael, Karen. *Army Times: Screenings Needed 4 Months after Redeployment,* (January 7, 2005).

Williams, Tom, editor. (1987). *Post-Traumatic Stress Disorders: A Handbook for Clinicians. Appendix I.* Cincinnati, OH.: Disabled American Veterans.

New Idea Magazine: Brainoes Down Under, March 3, 1987.

(Nov. 1, 2004) *Seattle Post-Intelligencer.*

Matsakis, Aphrodite., (1992). *I Can't Get Over It: A Handbook for Trauma Survivors.* Oakland, CA.: New Harbinger.

Peck, Scott M., (1987). *The Different Drum*, New York, NY.: Simon and Schuster.

http://www.globalsecurity.org *Balad Airbase*

van der Kolk, Bessell, (1988b). "The Trauma Spectrum: The Interaction of Biological and Social Events in the Genesis of the Trauma Response." *Journal of Traumatic Stress* 1:3.

KNOWING ASLAN

AN ENCOUNTER
WITH THE
LION OF NARNIA

THOMAS WILLIAMS

W PUBLISHING GROUP

A Division of Thomas Nelson Publishers
Since 1798

www.wpublishinggroup.com

Published by W Publishing Group, a Division of Thomas Nelson, Inc., P.O. Box 141000, Nashville, Tennessee 37214.

W Publishing Group books may be purchased in bulk for educational, business, fundraising, or sales promotional use. For information, please e-mail SpecialMarkets@ThomasNelson.com.

Library of Congress Cataloging-in-Publication Data

Williams, T. M. (Thomas Myron), 1941-
    Knowing Aslan : an encounter with the lion of
Narnia / Thomas Williams.
        p. cm.
Includes bibliographical references.
    ISBN 0-8499-0494-3
    1. Lewis, C. S. (Clive Staples), 1898-1963.
Chronicles of Narnia. 2. Children's stories, English—
History and criticism. 3. Christian fiction, English—
History and criticism. 4. Fantasy fiction, English—
History and criticism. 5. Narnia (Imaginary place) 6.
God in literature. I. Title.
    PR6023.E926C53984 2005
    823'.912—dc22

                                          2005015816

Printed in the United States of America

05 06 07 08 09 OPM 9 8 7 6 5 4 3

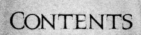

CONTENTS

Chapter One

OUR MISUNDERSTOOD GOD

WHO IS ASLAN? YOU KNOW, OF COURSE, IF you've seen the movie or read the book that he's the magnificent Lion in C. S. Lewis's *The Lion, the Witch and the Wardrobe.* But not everyone who has met Aslan picks up on who he really is. Perhaps this describes you. You may have loved the story but missed the deeper significance of the Lion. If so, let me tell you a little more about Narnia and Aslan.

Early in the story four English children

1

accidentally enter a parallel world—the archaic kingdom of Narnia—through an enchanted wardrobe. When a Narnian beaver meets them and says he must lead them to Aslan, the very sound of the name gives the children extraordinary feelings: "Peter felt suddenly brave and adventurous. Susan felt as if some delicious smell or some delightful strain of music had just floated by her. And Lucy got the feeling you have when you wake up in the morning and realize that it is the beginning of the holidays or the beginning of summer."[1]

The children learn that Aslan is actually the Lord and God of the Narnian world. When they meet him, they utterly adore him, and it's easy to see why: The Lion is the very picture of love. Throughout all seven of Lewis's books known as *The Chronicles of Narnia*, Aslan shows warm affection to them and to the creatures of the kingdom. He protects them, rescues them, fights for them, teaches them, weeps with them, plays with them, kisses them, laughs with them, and even dies for them. It's easy to love Aslan, and everyone in Narnia does. (Well, not *everyone*. But we'll talk about that later.)

"OK, I see where you're going," you may say. "You're telling me that Aslan is really God. It's a nice fantasy, but it's all wishful thinking. The God that's been shown to me is nothing like Aslan."

I understand that your picture of God may be far different from the Lion of Narnia. You may see God as anything but warm and loving. You may see God as highly demanding, strict, and judgmental, giving us a list of rigid rules and watching us through surveillance cameras with a

What you would like
from God is what Aslan offers the
Narnians—real concern, tender care,
unconditional love,
and deep joy.

frown on his face as he records every misdeed in a thick book. You may believe that God will love us only if we perform well. He has high standards and low tolerance; if we fail to toe the line, he writes us off. We may manage to avoid hell and squeak into heaven, but only if we rigidly follow his commandments and keep up our church attendance like a released felon reporting to a parole officer.

You may blame God for your tragedies and troubles. Why did God let your dear loved one die? Or why didn't he keep you from going bankrupt, or from suffering with this horrible disease or crippling injury or divorce or family estrangement? You may reason that either God does not care, or he is not powerful enough to do anything about your troubles. Either way, he's not what you want in a God.

What you would like from God is what Aslan offers the Narnians—real concern, tender care, unconditional love, and deep joy. So when you watch the movie or read one of the Narnian stories, it's little wonder if you sigh and wish your God were like that.

I'm happy to tell you that these common ideas so many people have about God are gross distortions, even libelous. You have been misled. The real God *is* like the fictional Aslan. Very much like Aslan. Or more accurately, Aslan is very much like the real God. In fact, one of the reasons C. S. Lewis created Aslan was to correct our image of God and show us the truth about him. Lewis understood our negative feelings—even resentment—toward God. He had been there. A believer in childhood, he turned to atheism when his mother died before his tenth birthday, destroying the happy life of his family. In his twenty years as an atheist, he found modern religion a big turnoff.

After his return to Christianity, Lewis created Aslan and wrote *The Lion, the Witch and the Wardrobe* to reveal the real truth about God without triggering all the defenses we raise against religion. So let's go into the story and see what Aslan shows us about God.

Chapter Two

THE TROUBLE WITH EDMUND

WE'LL BEGIN WITH EDMUND, THE THIRD OF the four young siblings in the story. I don't know what was wrong with that boy. Maybe he was affected by the "middle-child syndrome." Lacking the status of the older Peter and Susan, or the cuteness and attention of the younger Lucy, maybe he felt left out, insignificant, overlooked. Maybe that's why he became such a bully and pest.

After seeing Lucy enter the enchanted wardrobe, he sneaks into it alone and finds himself in Narnia. Aslan has long been absent from the country, and an old enemy, the White Witch, has taken over the land and frozen it under permanent winter. She is acutely aware of an ancient prophecy that predicts her end when four human children sit on the thrones of Narnia. So when she encounters Edmund wandering through the woods, alarms go off in her head. She entices the boy with his favorite treat, Turkish delight, and gets him to reveal that he has a brother and two sisters. Four human children—she must do away with them. She promises Edmund more of the treat if he will bring his siblings to her. She says she intends to make him a king in Narnia, and he needs his brother and sisters as his courtiers. He agrees to bring them. He will do anything for more Turkish delight. He thinks he has come into a really good deal. He can lord it over his siblings and have anything he desires, including all the candy he can stuff into his mouth. He doesn't realize, however, that the candy is enchanted, and anyone who tastes it will crave more and will go on craving and eating it until he kills himself.

Soon afterward, when the four children enter Narnia together, Edmund tries to maneuver them toward the witch's castle. But the good beaver intercepts them, warns them of the witch, and escorts them to Aslan. On the way, however, Edmund sneaks off to find the witch, intent on betraying the others.

CRAVINGS OUT OF CONTROL

We all tend to be like Edmund, with an "it's all about me" mind-set that drives us to satisfy

11

cravings we can't resist, even when they become destructive and deadly. No doubt you've experienced it firsthand. Perhaps at first you used your credit card just to buy a few things you had always wanted. But after maxing out three cards, you still can't stop spending. Or maybe you try every fad diet that comes along but stick with each for hardly a week before a burger binge balloons your weight again. Maybe you've tried to quit smoking many times—but each time started up again after only a few days. Or maybe you thought you could quit drinking, but even after losing your job and your spouse, you still reach for the bottle. Maybe you're a workaholic who has vowed to spend more time with your family, but soon your job sucks you back into endless nights at the office. Maybe you have vowed never to look at porn again, but you still sneak out to the triple-X arcade. Maybe your boss has told you that if you lose temper with an employee one more time, you can clean out your desk.

I'm sure you know the problem. First-hand. It's a condition all of us share. We are all like Edmund, loaded with weaknesses we can't handle, and we wonder, *Why did God make us so vulnerable to our cravings?*

THE WAY WE'RE MEANT TO BE

The question reveals one big misunder-standing about God. He didn't make us this way. The first humans he created were beautiful, healthy, and perfect. They were in complete control of all their desires. No problems overeating, overdrinking, over-spending, or overdoing anything. They were in perfect harmony with nature, each other, and God.

Why were they so perfect? For one thing, everything God made was perfect simply because that is the way God works. All nature as God first created it was fresh, lush, beautiful, in perfect balance, and utterly benign. As the crowning act of creation, God created man and woman. The Bible tells us that with them he went one step further than mere perfection and created them "in His own image."[1]

What does this mean? Well, you know how it is when you create anything dear to your heart; you tend to put something of yourself into it. It's said that novelists model every character in their stories after themselves to some degree. A house, a garden, a painting, or even a business will in some way reflect its creator's personality. It's the same with God. He made the first man and woman, Adam and Eve, to be like himself,

14

not only perfect in every way, but also in perfect control of themselves and everything around them.

God placed these perfect humans in charge of his perfect world, giving them the exalted honor of being his "deputy gods" on the earth.[2] He placed them in the luscious paradise known to us as Eden, where they lived a life in blissful harmony with God, untouched by pain, sickness, trouble, or death.

You know how you tend to fall in love with the things you create? Many artists have certain paintings they will not sell. Entrepreneurs who create businesses usually devote their lives to them. We dearly love the children we bring into the world. The same is true of God. He was in love with Adam and Eve. He delighted in the gorgeous couple loving and cavorting in the green woods. Genesis indicates that he was their companion, walking with them in the garden in the cool of the evening.[3] Adam and Eve had a world of beauty and wonder, they had each other, and all of it filled them with unbounded joy. But their greatest love and delight was God himself. No gap, no misunderstanding, no alienation existed between God and them. This is the way God created things to be.

Obviously, things have changed since then. Drastically. In the next chapter we will see how we became less like Adam and more like Edmund.

Chapter Three

HOW THINGS WENT WRONG

WHAT WENT WRONG IN EDEN? HOW DID WE get from the perfect world of Adam and Eve to this death-and-disease-ravaged world filled with people like Edmund who will betray his own brother and sisters for another fix of candy? The answer begins with the fact that God did not put us humans on autopilot. Instead of making Adam and Eve puppets or robots or controlling them with instinct like the animals, God gave them complete freedom. They could freely choose whether to live in harmony with God or reject him. He gave the couple one simple command—a prohibition to eat a certain fruit—to signify whether they would choose to follow the path God had designed for them or try to find happiness in their own way. They might have remained in the blissful Garden of Eden forever had not the malicious enemy Satan tempted them into eating the fruit. Their first bite signaled that they were rejecting God and choosing to go it alone.

How did God react? If I had been God, I know what I would have said: "Those ungrateful wretches! After all I've done for them, they turn their backs on me. If that's the way they're going to act, good riddance!" But God's response was nothing like that. He was heartbroken. He felt the way you feel when a beloved mate or child rejects you. But he sadly honored their choice. He got out of their lives and let them go their own way.

As you can see, it was Adam and Eve who created the gap between God and humankind. God didn't do it; he didn't want it, and it grieved him. But to honor their freedom, he had to withdraw and become invisible and inaudible, giving them the independence they demanded.

Adam and Eve hadn't a clue as to what their disobedience and rejection of God had set in motion. Just as the White Witch turned Narnia into a place where it was "always winter and never Christmas,"[1] Satan put the world under the dominion of evil. Storms, floods, weeds, disease, ruin, rot, and death infected the earth. All the evils that plague us today invaded the lives of Adam and Eve and their descendants—disharmony, hate, greed, murder, envy, pride, lust, shame, guilt, and lack of self-control. Thus contaminated, they became what the Bible calls sinners.

What is a sinner? A sinner is one who rejects God and turns to self as one's own authority. That's rebellion. And every son of Adam and daughter of Eve has done it. No exceptions. The Bible tells us that "all have sinned and fall short of the glory of God."[2] When Adam and Eve sinned—ate the forbidden fruit—they took the entire race down with them. We inherited that desire to rebel against authority, to have our cravings satisfied, to do only what we want to do and please only ourselves.

You've seen the symptoms. You know people who can't hold a job because they can't stand being told what to do. You know others who can't stay in a marriage because they can't give up their own wants for the sake of another. You know teenagers who long for the day they can get out on their own and do whatever they want. Don't you sometimes feel it yourself? Be honest. Don't you sometimes chafe at having to do what you ought to do instead of what you want— at having a boss control your life forty hours a week and a wife, husband, or kids invading your space the rest of the time? You're not alone. We all resist authority, and we all want to please ourselves—to have what we want when we want it. We are like Adam and Eve and Edmund, rebels wanting no one to tell us what to do and filled with almost irresistible cravings to please ourselves at all costs.

THE DOOM OF THE DEEP MAGIC

Edmund informs the witch that his brother and sisters have come to Narnia. But instead of rewarding his treachery with the promised Turkish delight, she enslaves him and prepares to execute him to foil the prophecy of her doom. Although the Narnians rescue Edmund, the witch claims the right to take his life. The boy is a traitor who has rejected Aslan, so he belongs to her. Edmund's horrified siblings protest, but Aslan affirms the witch's right to take their brother's life. The ancient Deep Magic from the Dawn of Time decrees that all traitors be turned over to her to be killed.

Our world has a law exactly like Narnia's Deep Magic: "The wages of sin is death,"[3] the Bible tells us. As in Narnia, the law in our world is that all traitors and rebels shall be given over to the evil power for destruction. And there's more to death than just the cessation of bodily life that we witness when a person dies. Sinners—those who reject

God—are doomed to remain in death, forever separated from God. That's the doom we've inherited from our first parents—a doom that fell on us because we disconnected from God. We thought we could take control of our own lives, but without God at the helm, our desires took control of us and spun us out of control. And there's no stoping us short of destruction.

In Edmund we see clearly how yielding to temptation leads to destruction. The desire leads to the taste, the taste leads to lust for more, and the lust for more leads to loss of self-control and destruction. As the Bible explains, "Temptation comes from the lure of our own evil desires. These evil desires lead to evil actions, and evil actions lead to death."[4] Sin is like a deadly addiction. We go on grasping for a pleasure even when it becomes destructive. It enslaves the will, becoming almost impossible to resist in spite of the consequences.

The witch's temptation of Edmund in Narnia is the same kind that we face today. No matter the details and circumstances, Satan's message is identical: "Get out from under God's thumb; take charge of your own life; satisfy all your desires." Perhaps you've got a shot at your lifelong ambition of being a company vice president, but it means hiding certain corporate activities from clients and auditors. You want the job so badly you can taste it, so you rationalize. Can God really expect anyone to turn down such a once-in-a-lifetime opportunity? After all, everyone hides some little something. And on your new salary you can triple your church contribution. Perhaps you're in love with the man in the next office, but he's married, though unhappily. Can God really expect you to live a life of hopeless longing just because of the technicality of a mistaken wedding vow? Surely you have a right to happiness. Satan urges you to go for it. Put aside God's irksome rules. Take matters into your own hands, create your own destiny, and satisfy those desires.

Our inability to resist such temptations shows our addiction to sin. We do things we cannot help, say words we wish we could take back, commit acts we wish we hadn't, yield where we wish we had resisted. We try to change—to hold our tempers, to quit smoking or drinking, to spend more time with our wives, husbands, or kids. And we may succeed for a while, but soon that old habit creeps back in. We see it clearly when we make New Year's resolutions. How long before they're all broken and our cravings take over again? We can't help it. God gave us our desires to lead us to joy, but since we rejected him, we can no longer manage them, and now they lead us to lust and addiction. We are all rebels deserving death. Eternal death.

We need help. Desperately.

Chapter Four

THE RESCUE

PETER, SUSAN, AND LUCY PLEAD WITH ASLAN to do something about Edmund's execution. Can't he undo the Deep Magic that demands their brother's death? The answer is no. The foundational laws of Narnia cannot be broken. But as the children despair, the Lion confers privately with the witch. When the conference ends, he announces that she has forfeited her claim on Edmund's life. The children are overjoyed.

That night after everyone has bedded

The great Lion of Narnia is dead.
He has given his own life
to save Edmund.

down, Aslan leaves the camp. With great heaviness of heart, he walks toward an ancient sacred mound. Susan and Lucy, who cannot sleep, follow at a distance. The White Witch and her monsters await the Lion. They seize him, bind him, insult him, and beat him as he silently submits. Then they heave him onto the great Stone Table, where the witch raises her knife and slays him. From their hiding place, the two girls gape in horror. The great Lion of Narnia is dead. He has given his own life to save Edmund.

THE FREE GIFT

What Aslan did for Edmund reflects exactly what God did for us. After Adam and Eve rebelled, taking down the entire human race, we all deserved death. We had failed to be what God created us to be. But God was in love with us, and the thought of spending eternity without us was more than he could bear. "I'm going after them," he said, in effect. "It doesn't matter what they've done or said; I love them too much to let them go. Whatever it takes, I'm going to get them back."

Whatever it takes meant death. To save us, God would have to die in our place. It didn't deter him for a moment. He loved us that much. God came to earth as the man called Jesus and died, nailed to a Roman executioner's cross. And because he did that for us, we, like Edmund in Narnia, are rescued from death. Of course, we still have to die physically; the doom we inherited from Adam can't be undone. But Jesus' sacrifice rescues us from eternal death—death that puts us forever outside the loving presence of God. As the Bible tells us, "Everyone dies because all of us are related to Adam, the first man. But all who are related to Christ, the other man, will be given new life."[1]

Now this is very good news. The best possible news. Because without Jesus' death to pay the price for our rebellion and forgive us for it, we would have no escape from the doom of the law that says rebels against God deserve eternal death. In fact, this news may seem too good to be true. When a telemarketing call interrupts your dinner to offer a free vacation trip to Cancún, you know there's a catch. Strings are attached somewhere, ready to entangle you in a lifetime of payments. You say "no thanks" and hang up. Nothing is free. So when you hear that God died to free you from death, you may wonder, *OK, what's the catch?*

There is no catch. Or if there is, it's God who was caught by his love. What he did for us has no strings attached. He takes the hit and forgives our sins.

"SURELY HE CAN'T FORGIVE WHAT I'VE DONE"

You may have trouble believing in God's free offer, because you think you have sinned beyond what he can forgive. *He may forgive others*, you may think, *but he could never forgive what I've done.* Maybe you've done some pretty terrible things. Maybe you've wounded people, used people, driven them away, or worse. Maybe you hide a shameful habit, a lifestyle secret, or you've committed a deed so terrible you can't even talk about it. Maybe you have even caused someone's death or ruin. You can't forgive yourself; how can God possibly forgive you?

Have you done worse than Jesus' friend and disciple Peter? They had worked together, side by side, for three years, and yet when Jesus was arrested and dragged to judgment, Peter abandoned him, denying that he even knew Jesus—not once, but three times. Have you done worse than the early church leader Paul of Tarsus? He had made a career of persecuting and executing innocent Christians. Have you done worse than King David? He voyeuristically ogled a naked woman bathing, sneaked her into his chamber, committed adultery with her, and when she became pregnant, he had her husband killed so he could marry her to cover up his sin. Yet God died for each of these terrible sinners, and they accepted the free gift of his forgiveness.

Imagine a town in which an association of local doctors controls all medical practice.

One day a new young doctor arrives. He does not join the association (in fact, they would never accept him because his credentials are not from the right medical school). He doesn't even set up an office but, unlike the association physicians, does all his healing work by making house calls. Also unlike the other physicians, he heals not only those who have money or health insurance, but also those too poor to pay. From them he takes whatever they can afford—tomatoes from their garden, a jar of home-canned peaches, or a neck scarf knitted by a grateful mother. And he heals many diseases that the association doctors can't touch.

The association doctors lose none of their business—the wealthy people still come to them—but they grow envious of this young upstart's success. They decide to shut him down. They hire spies to pump information from his patients, trying to figure out how he works. They find that many of his methods violate association standards. They warn him to cease such practices, but he ignores them and goes about his healing.

One day the body of a farmer is brought in from his field, obviously the victim of sunstroke. The association doctors know the young physician had nothing to do with the death, but because he had recently cured the farmer's ulcer, they see their chance to do him in. They arrest him and charge him with malpractice. At the trial they bribe witnesses to lie, and the doctor is convicted and hung.

Can these association doctors be forgiven? This little story is much like what happened to Jesus, and we find the answer in what he said as he was hanging on the cross. He forgave those who executed him.[2]

In fact, that was the whole purpose of his death — to forgive those who don't deserve it and have no means of clearing themselves. If it can work for the people who killed Jesus, it can work for you and me. You can't fall beyond his love.

Maybe there's no free lunch, but there is free forgiveness. That is, it's free to you and me. It cost a terrible price, but it has already been paid. Willingly.

Chapter Five

A CAUSE FOR CELEBRATION

WHAT ASLAN DOES NEXT IN NARNIA CATCHES everyone by surprise. After the witch executes him, Susan and Lucy stay by his body, weeping. As dawn breaks, they walk about to keep warm. Suddenly the Stone Table on which the Lion was killed splits in two, and they turn to see him alive, larger and more glorious than ever.

Then comes a second surprise:

A mad chase began. Round and round
the hill-top he led them, now hope-
lessly out of their reach, now letting
them almost catch his tail, now diving
between them, now tossing them in the
air with his huge and beautifully vel-
veted paws and catching them again,
and now stopping unexpectedly so that
all three of them rolled over together in
a happy laughing heap of fur and arms
and legs. It was such a romp as no one
has ever had except in Narnia.[1]

After the tragedy of execution and the
triumph of resurrection, the last thing we
expect from the great Lion is cavorting
with a couple of kids in the morning grass.
We expect him to display majesty, exulta-
tion, power, and perhaps joy, but surely a
kind of noble, high-minded joy; not a *romp*.

But Aslan doesn't hold back; he romps with extravagant joy. And there's good reason for it.

Just as Aslan came back from the dead, so did Jesus. Three days after his crucifixion, he burst from the tomb and appeared alive and healthier than ever to hundreds of witnesses. His resurrection shows us that the power of evil and death is broken. It shows us that God is stronger than death. He has defeated it. His resurrection also shows us—and the New Testament promises—that we, too, will be resurrected after we die.[2] All our flaws will be corrected. We will be beautiful and perfect, both in body and soul. No more pain or death. We will be like Adam and Eve in Eden; our companionship with God will be restored. No more gap. Ever since Adam and Eve sinned, God's whole purpose with us has been

restoration. He doesn't intend to let Satan
ruin his good creation. He will put all of
it—including you and me—back like he
intended in the beginning. That is a cause
for celebration—a cause for enormous joy—
good cause for a romp.

LIVING IN EXTRAVAGANT JOY

The idea that Christians should be long-
faced and wary of too much joy is outra-
geous nonsense. Christians should enjoy
life more than unbelievers. They are free
from the guilt of sin and free to enjoy all the
blessings God offers. He gave us those "thou
shalt not" commandments, not to keep us
from pleasure, but to tell us how to manage
our desires in order to achieve joy.

Narnia under Aslan is a merry land of
joy, feasting, dancing, jesting, and laughter.

Narnia simply reflects what we find in the Bible. King David was so joyful over the return of the ark of the covenant to Israel that he leapt and whirled at the head of the parade that brought it into Jerusalem. Jesus didn't require his disciples to fast as the self-righteous religious leaders demanded. He wanted them joyful while he was with them. Jesus told funny stories (straining out a gnat while swallowing a camel, a log hanging from the eye of someone trying to clean a speck of dust from the eye of another, a camel squeezing through the eye of a needle). He was always attending parties (the gospel accounts repeatedly show him at feasts). He partied so much that the joy killers of his day called him a glutton and a wino. In fact, one of his miracles was to make a hundred gallons of wine for a wedding party.

"Joy is the serious business of Heaven,"[3] C. S. Lewis wrote elsewhere. Joy is what God is about. Aslan's joyful romp with the children shows God's intention for all of us. Jesus died so that we could escape the misery Satan inflicted and experience the joy God intended. Wild, extravagant joy.

LOOKING FOR JOY IN ALL THE WRONG PLACES

We will experience joy fully when we are resurrected to new life. But the good news is that we can experience it even now in this world that Adam and Eve messed up. It's sometimes more of a challenge, of course. In fact, your life may be such that you find little reason for joy. Failures, broken relationships, tragedies, illnesses, or other woes may have robbed you of it. Perhaps you feel that if you could only get your life together and find a measure of security, significance, and love, joy would come your way. But you just can't seem to get there. Maybe you've tried to find significance in a company title and a corner office. Maybe you've looked for security in sound investments, retirement funds, and paid-off mortgages. Maybe you've reached out for love in ways good or bad—permanent relationships, temporary liaisons, friends, pets, organizations, fame, or even church memberships. Whatever you lock in on—family, career, friendship, romance, sex, food, drink, houses, cars, books, movies, sports, or hobbies—it will fail to give you what you're looking for, because the true source of your joy lies beyond these immediate fixes.

Blaise Pascal put his finger on the problem. He recognized that all human desires

Joy is the serious
business of Heaven.

are the diffused rays of a single desire caused by a "God-shaped vacuum" inside each human heart. Ever since Adam and Eve rejected God, we've felt this empty hole aching to be filled, and we spend our lives trying in every way possible to fill it. But only one thing can fill it: God himself. Only by restoring that lost relationship with him will you ever find true significance, security, and love. Only when you experience God's love—a love that's already there, waiting for you—will you experience real joy.

HOW CAN I
EXPERIENCE GOD'S LOVE?

We fall in love with Aslan because he shows his love so vividly. He romps with his Narnians, lets them ride on him, kisses them, instructs them, leads them, protects them, embraces them, corrects them, and even dies for them. It's easy to love a God like this, but perhaps not so easy to love a God you can't see, hear, or hug.

We no longer have God as our visible, audible companion as did Adam and Eve in Eden or Jesus' disciples when he was here on earth. But God is with us as a living Spirit, working for us behind the scenes and within the lives of Christians, even though he is presently invisible to us. He loves you every bit as dearly as Aslan loves his Narnians, and you can experience his love and know that it's real.

One tangible evidence of that love is the world he created, filled with delights meant for our joy—the beauty of nature, the care of a friend, the love of a wife or husband or child, and the simple but overlooked pleasures of everyday existence. Every time you snuggle under a warm blanket on a cold night, God is loving you. Every time your daughter hugs you, she is passing on God's love. You find his love in the taste of a hot breakfast, the caress of a breeze, the tingling thrill of great music, the breathtaking beauty of a mountain, or in the devotion and affection of a pet. In spite of the blight and decay that Satan inflicted on the earth, all nature, all good relationships, all pleasurable experiences shout the message: God loves you and wants you to experience joy.

You can also know God's love when things are not going well. When the job ends, when the marriage fails, when a loved one dies, God grieves with you, just as Jesus wept at the tomb of his friend Lazarus.[4] He is invisible and inaudible, but your spirit can interact with his. You can know that he is there; share your grief with him, and he will give you comfort and strength. This continual awareness of God is a kind of ongoing prayer that will draw you closer to him and increase your sense of his presence. Practice this and you will come to love Jesus. And he will become as real to you as Aslan is to the Narnians.

Think about the greatest love you have ever known. It is only a shadow of the love that God has for you. When this life ends and you finally see him, you will know that you have just met the love of your life. You will know that he is what you really have been longing for in every desire you ever had.

Chapter Six

BEGINNING THE JOURNEY

GOD IS NOW PREPARING HEAVEN FOR US, the beautiful country we reach at death. Contrary to popular images, heaven is not an elaborate retirement center—an insipid place of fluffy clouds, white gowns, halos, and harps where you will be bored to tears. Heaven will be as the last book in *The Chronicles of Narnia* reveals it and the book of Revelation hints: a restored and perfected earth.[1] As Lewis shows us in Narnia, we will not be ghosts in that country; we

*If you have not begun the journey
to your true country, let me urge you
to begin it now.*

will have real bodies restored to their pain-proof, age-proof, death-proof perfection and beautiful beyond imagining. We will fulfill our original role as God's creative deputies. Narnia shows heaven to be a place like Eden, lush with trees, grass, mountains, and water-falls, where we will live forever a life of meaningful activity, bathed in ecstatic joy.[2]

As one creature said when he reached the Narnian heaven—the restored and perfected Narnia: "I have come home at last! This is my real country!"[3] When we arrive in heaven, we will know it to be our real country where we will feel completely at home forever.

THE COMPANY
OF FELLOW STRUGGLERS

If you have not begun the journey to your real country, let me urge you to begin it now. But don't try to travel alone. Loners are vulnerable and easily discouraged. Get with others who know the way and can help you get there. Many who have invited God to fill their God-shaped vacuums have formed a company we call the church. Like Narnians committed to Aslan, this company is committed to following Jesus more closely and loving him more deeply.

You may be eager to follow Jesus but less excited about hooking up with a church. You may think of church as a stuffy place filled with hypocrites and self-righteous prigs. You may think you can be a perfectly good Christian without it.

If the church seems full of hypocrites, it's because of a common misunderstanding of what church is about. People tend to think Christians should be better than others and have their lives together. But as someone has aptly said, the church is not a showplace for saints; it's a hospital for sinners. It's not a place for good people to strut their stuff, but a place for forgiven people to help one another draw closer to God. Christians are far from perfect. We have turned back to God, but we still slip into selfish mode. The big advantage of being in a church is that when these slips occur we have fellow strugglers to help us get back on track.

In the church we develop a sort of double-level vision that enables us to see two things at once: We see in one another the image of God—what he intended us to be and what we will become, and at the same time we also see the weaknesses that mar the image. We are all like alcoholics, addicted to sin in general and each to some sin in particular. Awareness of this darker side does not cause us to condemn one another, but rather to see in the mirror of our neighbor our own fallen condition. In each other we see how desperately we need God and how dependent we are on one another. Church is a safe place where we can lay our weakness on the table and get help from one another in resisting overwhelming temptations.

If you're serious about following Jesus, find a church and look for fellow strugglers who will welcome you with open arms and enfold you within their family. Immerse yourself in the church's timeless rituals of baptism and communion, and enjoy the fellowship and support of fellow believers as you travel toward your ultimate destination—the joy of fully restored fellowship with the God who loves you more dearly than heaven itself.

OPEN THE DOOR

Jesus loves you so much that he died for you, and he longs for a relationship with you. But you still have free will, and he will not force himself upon you. If you choose to remain apart from him, he will be heartbroken, but he will honor your choice. Until you willingly come to him and accept his sacrifice and forgiveness, he cannot free you from the fatal doom that sin has imposed on you. He yearns for you to take that step, but you must do it willingly.

He knocks at the door of your heart. If you are ready to open yourself to him, you might find it helpful to pray the following prayer:

Dear God, thank you so much for loving me. Thank you for dying in my place. Thank you for forgiving my sins, offering me a life of peace, free from guilt, and filled with joy. I open my heart for you to come in. I commit my life to you. Give me your Spirit to make me all you created me to be, so that my life may reflect your nature. I pray this prayer through the name of your loving Son, Jesus Christ. Amen.

If you prayed this prayer, you've taken an important first step. Now I urge you not to wait—don't put it off even for a moment—to find a church. Join the company. Get in step with the rest of us who are marching toward Aslan's country. I hope to meet you there someday.

May God bless you on your journey.

NOTES

CHAPTER 1
1. C. S. Lewis, *The Lion, the Witch and the Wardrobe* (1950; repr., New York: HarperCollins, 1978), 74-75.

CHAPTER 2
1. Genesis 1:27.
2. See Genesis 1:28–30.
3. Genesis 3:8.

CHAPTER 3
1. Lewis, *The Lion, the Witch and the Wardrobe*, 20.
2. Romans 3:23.
3. Romans 6:23.
4. James 1:14–15 (NLT).

CHAPTER 4
1. 1 Corinthians 15:22 (NLT).
2. Luke 23:34.

CHAPTER 5
1. Lewis, *The Lion, the Witch and the Wardrobe*, 179.
2. 1 Corinthians 15:52, 54.
3. C. S. Lewis, *Letters to Malcolm, Chiefly on Prayer* (New York: Harcourt, Brace & World, 1964), 93.
4. John 11:35.

CHAPTER 6
1. Revelation 21:1.
2. Romans 8:23.
3. C.S. Lewis, *The Last Battle* (1956; repr., New York: HarperCollins, 1983), 213.

ABOUT THE AUTHOR

THOMAS WILLIAMS' ten books include fiction, theology, and drama, among them *The Heart of the Chronicles of Narnia* and the Gold Medallion Award finalist *In Search of Certainty*, written with Josh McDowell. In addition to writing, Williams is a career designer and illustrator. His painting of C.S. Lewis hangs in the Wade Collection at Wheaton College. Tom and his wife, Faye, live in Granbury, Texas.